# FIRST AMENDMENT

## FOR BEGINNERS®

# FIRST AMENDMENT
## FOR BEGINNERS®

### BY MICHAEL J. LAMONICA
### ILLUSTRATED BY JEFF FALLOW

**FOR BEGINNERS®**

For Beginners LLC
30 Main Street, Suite 303
Danbury, CT 06810 USA
www.forbeginnersbooks.com

A For Beginners® Documentary Comic Book
Copyright © 2018

Cataloging-in-Publication information is available from the Library of Congress.

ISBN # 978-1-939994-74-5 Trade

Manufactured in the United States of America

For Beginners® and Beginners Documentary Comic Books® are published by
For Beginners LLC.

First Edition

10 9 8 7 6 5 4 3 2 1

*To Mylène and Louis-Étienne*

# FIRST AMENDMENT
## FOR BEGINNERS®

# CONTENTS

# INTRODUCTION

**F**EW STATEMENTS OF LAW AND GOVERNMENT INSPIRE as much passionate argument as the First Amendment to the US Constitution. In just 45 words, it acts as both the vanguard provision of the Bill of Rights—the "fixed star in our constitutional constellation," according to Justice Robert Jackson—and a political lightning rod that attracts controversy. While support for the First Amendment is in many ways one of the last remaining points of bipartisan consensus in America, the way in which we interpret its meaning remains hotly contested, touching on the perpetual question of how to balance the rights of the individual against the needs of society at large. This is not just a modern phenomenon. The fight over the First Amendment has been going on since its ratification in 1791.

The language of the First Amendment, written in less-than-crystal-clear 18th-century prose, reads:

*Congress shall make no law respecting an establishment of religion, or prohibiting the free exercise thereof; or abridging the freedom of speech, or of the press; or the right of the people peaceably to assemble, and to petition the Government for a redress of grievances.*

I

The text seems to raise more questions than provide answers. For instance: What exactly does it mean to "establish" a religion? Do I have the right to "exercise" my religious beliefs even if they violate the law? Is *all* speech protected, absolutely, all the time? Can the press publish *anything* it wants? Why does the First Amendment prohibit only Congress from restricting these rights? Does that mean my state or my boss at work can take away my freedom of speech?

The first part of this book begins to tackle these questions by exploring both the historical background of the First Amendment and the structure of the federal judiciary. Nothing is decided in a vacuum, and the Founding Fathers, for all their well-earned accolades, did not pull the First Amendment out of a tricorn hat. We will also look at how the Supreme Court got the power of judicial review (it's not mentioned in the Constitution) and figure out just what the heck the common law is anyway.

The second part of the book takes up the Establishment and Free Exercise clauses of the First Amendment, known collectively as the religion clauses. You might have heard of these passages as having something to do with the separation of church and state, but strangely enough, that phrase appears nowhere in the First Amendment either. Thus, we are left with questions such as: Does the Constitution allow for parochial school voucher programs, prayers during graduation ceremonies, or displays of the Ten Commandments on public property? And what do we do when the exercise of someone's religion conflicts with secular laws in some way? These are all tricky matters that the Supreme Court has struggled with over the years.

We have a winner!

1ST Amend.

In the third section, we explore freedom of speech and freedom of the press. Again, how can we know what and where the limits are when the wording of the First Amendment appears to be so absolute? Here we'll look at cases that ask whether it really is OK to shout "fire" in a crowded theater; to wear a T-shirt into a courthouse that says "F**K THE DRAFT!" (without the asterisks); to burn the American flag; to join the Communist Party; to sell nudie magazines; to ban Ku Klux Klan marches; or to publish confidential government secrets. We will also delve into some First Amendment questions that have taken on a new political life in recent years—namely, whether money equals speech, whether corporations are entitled to constitutional protections, and to what extent governments can regulate spending on political campaigns.

# A CRASH COURSE IN
# CONSTITUTIONAL LAW

# ◆ 1 ◆

## BRIEF HISTORY OF THE
## FIRST AMENDMENT

**B**EFORE WE DIVE INTO THE SUBSTANCE OF THE
First Amendment, let's start with a bit of history. The
Founding Fathers did not think up the ideas of freedom of
speech, religion, the press, and the rest all by themselves. Many of
these rights had a long pedigree extending back into the misty recesses
of the Middle Ages, and their implementation in the American system
was a far messier process than you might have learned about in high
school.

The foundational document for the First Amendment, and indeed the entire structure of constitutional government, is everyone's favorite piece of 13th-century moldy parchment: the **Magna Carta**, or Great Charter. That historic document arose out of a feudal dispute between England's King John I (of Robin Hood fame) and his power-hungry barons. In 1215, the beleaguered king was forced literally at sword-point to sign a piece of paper that placed limits on his power. The Magna Carta recognized the barons' right to a speedy trial and due process of law, protected them from arbitrary arrest and seizure of property, and forbade the king from levying taxes without consent. Far from being a liberal document that benefited the common man of the kingdom, the Magna Carta served the interests of the nobility—but at least it was a start!

The circulation of ideas brought about by the printing press and the renewal of conflict between the king, nobility, church, and parliament in 16th-century England led a newly educated class to reimagine the relationship between the individual and the state. To them, the Magna Carta embodied ancient freedoms and natural rights that all people possess and that government cannot infringe

upon. Parliament attempted to reign in the autocratic Charles I in 1628 by having him ratify the **Petition of Right**, which reaffirmed the Magna Carta and went further by both guaranteeing the right of habeas corpus and requiring consent of the owner to quarter troops in a private home (both also covered in the U.S. Constitution). Such measures were short-lived, however, as the outbreak of the English Civil War led to the beheading of Charles I in 1649, tabling for the time any further discussion about rights of speech, religion, assembly, and the press.

The English Civil War also had a formative impact on the North American colonies that would one day become the United States. The war fractured the colonies along political, religious, and geographical lines. Fiercely independent New Englanders favored the Puritanical Parliamentarians, and in 1641 the Massachusetts General Court passed a comprehensive Body of Liberties that guaranteed to all its people, for the first time, the rights to speech, assembly, and petition. Anglican colonies such as Virginia sided with the Crown, while Catholic Maryland saw the only battle of the English Civil War fought on American soil.

9

However, the seed of constitutionalism continued to blossom in the colonies both during and after the war, as the Maryland Toleration Act of 1649, the Rhode Island Charter of 1663, the West Jersey Concession and Agreement of 1676, and the Pennsylvania Charter of Privileges of 1683 all guaranteed religious freedom to Christians regardless of denomination—a very liberal gesture in its day!

The next formative event in First Amendment history was England's Glorious Revolution of 1688. Protestant parliamentarians, sick of the growing Catholicism and authoritarianism of King James II, decided to give him the royal boot and invited William of Orange, the leader of the Netherlands, to rule as a co-monarch with James's daughter, Mary. Upon the downfall of James II, revolts broke out throughout New England, New York, and Maryland, as disgruntled colonists forcibly ejected their hated royal governors. William and Mary, within months of taking power, ratified the most comprehensive grant of rights and freedoms to date: the **Bill of Rights of 1689**, the direct, lineal ancestor of the U.S. Bill of Rights.

This transatlantic conception of rights continued to evolve over the course of the 18th century, as the famous English jurist William Blackstone systematized and rationalized the messy English common law system (more about this in Chapter 2) in his magnum opus, *The Commentaries on the Laws of England* (1765—69). In that work, equal parts legal treatise and political polemic, Blackstone describes how the English common law system uniquely preserved the ancient rights and freedoms of the individual against absolute monarchy. Blackstone's masterful combination of law, politics, and philosophy was a hit among the new American elite. Over 2,000 copies were sold in Philadelphia alone, and Blackstone's hefty multivolume work graced the bookshelves of such colonial luminaries as Alexander Hamilton, John Jay, John Adams, John Marshall, and Thomas Jefferson.

Despite the growing belief that there were areas of individual life that should be free of state interference, the law in America lagged behind that principle for most of the 18th century. Many of the colonies continued to have official churches and afforded little protection to speech. The coming of the American Revolution began to change this dynamic. Under the direction of Thomas Jefferson, Virginia in 1776 became the first colony to pass a comprehensive Declaration of Rights, guaranteeing the "inherent rights" of freedom of speech, religion, and the press, among others. The exigencies of war quieted most philosophical discussion of individual rights for the time being, as the fledgling nation fought for its more immediate right to exist.

John Adams

The Treaty of Paris recognized American independence in 1783, and for the next six years the country continued to operate under the loose legal framework of the Articles of Confederation. That rickety structure proved unworkable, however, and the entire document was scrapped in favor of a new constitution. Representatives of the various states met for a constitutional convention in Philadelphia during the summer of 1787 and created a new governing document for the nation. Left out, at least at first, was an explicit guarantee of individual rights.

The failure to include a bill of rights in the original Constitution almost sank the entire venture. Some of the biggest names of the revolutionary cause came out against it and urged their state legislatures not to ratify the document. Alexander Hamilton argued forcefully in favor of ratification without a bill of rights, explaining in the *Federalist Papers* that such an explicit guarantee was not only unnecessary but also counterproductive. It could be viewed, he argued, as a grant of rights from the government—a grant that might be revoked at whim—and limit the rights retained by the people only to those enumerated in the document.

Hamilton's argument did not carry the day, and many states, including his own New York, refused to ratify the Constitution if it did not contain a bill of rights. Sam Adams and John Hancock of Massachusetts came up with a compromise: the states would ratify the Constitution but draw up a list of amendments for the first Congress to take up that would form the Bill of Rights. Virginia's James Madison led that campaign and drafted amendments explicitly guaranteeing rights contained in the Magna Carta, the English Bill of Rights, and the various colonial charters. Three-fourths of the states voted in

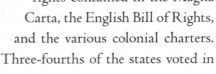

James
Madison

favor of the first ten amendments, and they became part of the Constitution on December 15, 1791.

The remarkable thing about this whole episode is that, after all the sound and fury over the necessity of a bill of rights, people seemed to forget about it almost as soon as it was adopted. The Supreme Court took a hands-off approach on the First Amendment until the 20th century. Why? We'll see in the chapters ahead.

# ✦ 2 ✦

# THE SUPREME COURT: MEN (AND WOMEN SINCE 1981) IN BLACK

**N**O EXAMINATION OF THE FIRST AMENDMENT WOULD be complete without an overview of the institution responsible for its interpretation: the United States Supreme Court. In this chapter, we will discuss why the Supreme Court has the final say on First Amendment issues, how a First Amendment case makes its way to the Supreme Court, and the ways in which the justices attempt to determine the meaning of its passages.

Justices of the Supreme Court at present :

**Article III of the Constitution** establishes the size, scope, organization, and role of the federal judiciary. It is amazingly short; you can fit most of the text on a cocktail napkin. Section 1 vests all judicial power in one Supreme Court and in "such inferior courts as the Congress may from time to time ordain and establish." This means that the only constitutionally mandated court is the U.S. Supreme Court. All lower federal courts are given the charming designation "creatures of Congress," meaning that they owe their existence to the legislature rather than to the Constitution. The rest of Section 1 requires that all federal judges hold their offices "during good behavior," meaning that they have life tenure unless impeached, and that Congress can't cut their pay—and that's it. All other important questions, even ones like how many judges should serve on the Supreme Court, are left unanswered.

Section 2 lays out the jurisdiction of the federal judiciary. Unlike state courts, which can hear any kinds of cases, federal courts can hear

16

Huh! Inferior courts.

Supreme Court

"Creatures of Congress"

only specific types of cases. The most important for our purposes are cases dealing with the Constitution, federal statutes (laws passed by Congress), or treaties. Section 2 also lists the types of cases in which the Supreme Court has "original jurisdiction" (lawsuits that originate in there)—cases involving ambassadors, other public ministers, and those in which a state is a party. Most of the cases that the Supreme Court hears are appeals from lower courts.

Supreme Court

Lower Courts

Nowhere in Article III is there any mention of **judicial review**, the Supreme Court's ability to strike down laws that conflict with the Constitution. In fact, judicial review is not mentioned anywhere in the entire Constitution. So if the awesome authority to declare laws unconstitutional isn't actually in the Constitution, where does it come from? The short answer is that the Court gave *itself* the power in the 1803 case of *Marbury v. Madison*. The long answer is a bit more complicated.

One of the defining features of the Anglo-American legal tradition—and essential to understanding the importance of *Marbury v. Madison*—is the **common law.** As opposed to statutory law (written by a legislative body), common law is the type made by judges when they issue a legal ruling on a specific case. In a common-law system, judicial decisions carry the force of law under the principle of stare decisis (Latin for "stand by the decision"). What this means is that judges tend to follow the rulings set by other judges, and lower courts are bound to follow the rulings of higher courts in their jurisdiction for all similar cases; this creates binding precedents. Since the Supreme Court is the highest court in the United States, its rulings are binding on the entire country.

## STATUTORY LAW:
Written law enacted by Congress...

## COMMON LAW:
Unwritten law enacted by judges (if an unprecedented case comes to court and a judge makes a decision, other judges will follow this ruling on how to deal with similar cases from then on)...

Are you ready to dive into the weeds of our first Supreme Court case? Let's set the scene: It's the year 1800 and the first political handover in U.S. history is about to take place. The Federalist Party, which had dominated politics in the 1790s, got wiped out in the last election, losing both houses of Congress and the presidency. Before handing over power to newly elected Thomas Jefferson and his Democratic-Republicans, President John Adams appointed a number of Federalist judges in the waning days of his administration. Upon taking the oath of office, President Jefferson tells his secretary of state, James Madison, not to deliver any judicial commissions that hadn't already gone out the door. William Marbury, one of the Federalist judges awaiting his commission, did what lawyers do best—he sued the Jefferson Administration.

This is where the case takes a curious twist. Marbury didn't file his lawsuit in any old court; he filed it at the U.S. Supreme Court. Remember that the Supreme Court has original jurisdiction only in a limited number of cases, and none of them applied here. But Marbury was asking the Court to issue an order directing the government to take a specific action (the Latin term is a "writ of mandamus"), and Congress had passed a law granting the Supreme Court the power to hear such petitions. Marbury believed he was simply following the rules.

Presiding over the case was Chief Justice John Marshall, a committed Federalist; Marbury must have liked his chances. Writing the opinion of the Court, the chief justice made short work of the issue at hand. Yes, Marbury was entitled to his commission, Marshall wrote. But he didn't stop there. The chief justice went on to ask whether the Supreme Court was the right place for Marbury to file his lawsuit. While Congress had passed a law authorizing the Supreme Court to hear such cases, the Constitution granted no such authority. So Chief Justice Marshall had a decision to make: either uphold the statute, implicitly saying that laws passed by Congress can override the Constitution, or do something truly unprecedented by invalidating a law passed by Congress and signed by the president.

Marshall went about his task brilliantly. He started with the proposition that "[i]t is emphatically the province and duty of the Judicial Department to say what the law is" and that "[i]f two laws conflict with each other, the courts must decide on the operation of each." On that basis, Marshall framed the case as a contest between the Constitution and a statute, where only one side could prevail. Citing his oath to uphold the Constitution and the text of the Supremacy Clause (Article VI, Clause 2), which establishes the Constitution as the supreme law of the land, Marshall was duty bound to rule in favor of the Constitution and strike down the offending portion of the statute. Thus, Marbury lost his suit and John Marshall established the Supreme Court as the Constitution's ultimate arbiter.

Almost as soon as John Marshall gave the Supreme Court the

awesome power of judicial review, however, he rendered it mostly toothless in the 1833 case of *Barron v. Baltimore*. Here, the Court held that the Bill of Rights applies only to the actions of the federal government and not state governments. This is why states in the early republic were allowed to maintain official churches, to take property without paying compensation, to imprison their citizens without trial, and to ban abolitionist speech, all without violating the Constitution.

Things began to change after the Civil War. The Thirteenth, Fourteenth, and Fifteenth Amendments were made specifically applicable to the states. The **Fourteenth Amendment** in particular marked a legal revolution, declaring explicitly:

*No State shall . . . deprive any person of life, liberty, or property, without due process of law; nor deny to any person within its jurisdiction the equal protection of the laws.*

Starting with the 1897 case of *Chicago, Burlington & Quincy Railroad Co. v. City of Chicago*, the Supreme Court began to interpret this to mean that certain fundamental rights in the Bill of Rights apply to the states through a legal doctrine called **incorporation.**

Now that we understand the Supreme Court's power of judicial review and its common law authority, let's turn to the question of how a First Amendment case makes its way to that body's colonnaded doorstep. A good starting point is to recognize that the Constitution protects a person's rights against infringement *only by the government.* This point can't be stressed strongly enough. Regardless of what you might hear from coworkers or read in blog posts, a private person or organization can *never* violate your constitutional rights.

A constitutional case begins in either a lower federal court or a state court. We don't need to get too bogged down with procedure, but it's good to have a basic understanding of the structure of the judiciary to understand future cases. Federal trial courts are called **U.S. District Courts**, and intermediate federal appellate courts are called **U.S. Circuit Courts**. The entire country is divided up geographically, so that federal courts hear cases from within their respective regions. Standing above them all is the U.S. Supreme Court. Outside the federal system, individual states also have their own systems of trial, intermediate appellate, and supreme courts.

SUPREME COURT

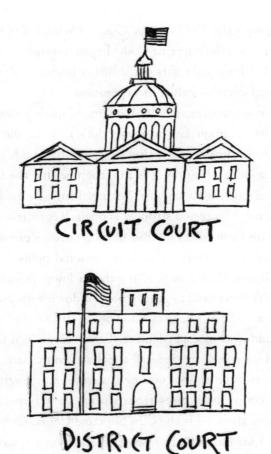

CIRCUIT COURT

DISTRICT COURT

The U.S. Supreme Court is also special because it gets to choose what cases it wants to hear. If you want the Supreme Court to hear your appeal, you need to petition it for what's called a **writ of certiorari**. The justices (well, their law clerks) comb through thousands of petitions to find the most weighty and meritorious cases to hear. The Court takes on only 80-100 cases each year, making the acceptance rate about 1%. And if your case is one of the lucky winners that actually manages to get in front of the justices, how do they rule on it? Since the text of the First Amendment contains few specific guidelines, two key factors determine how the Court resolves a case: the standard of review and the judicial philosophy of each judge.

The **standard of review** determines how closely the court will scrutinize the challenged statute. The two main standards of review are "rational basis" and "strict scrutiny." Under **rational basis review**, the court will approve a statute if it is rationally related to advancing a legitimate state interest in some way. This is a highly lenient standard; if the court uses it, the government usually wins. **Strict scrutiny review** does the exact opposite. Under that standard, the court will approve a statute only if it is absolutely necessary to accomplish a compelling state interest. Here the burden has shifted to the government; the dual requirement of absolute necessity and the need for a compelling (super-important) interest means that when the court employs strict scrutiny, the government usually loses. "Intermediate scrutiny" tests fall somewhere between the two extremes of rational basis and strict scrutiny. What factors apply in each test and how the individual justices weigh the interests at play tend to correlate with their judicial philosophies.

There are two major schools of constitutional interpretation, with most judges inclining more toward one side or the other. One school is known as **originalism.** Judges who follow this approach believe that the Constitution should be interpreted based either on the intent of the Founders or on the commonly held meaning of the words at that time. Originalists tend to favor categorical approaches that draw bright lines between constitutional and unconstitutional actions, and they are reluctant to expand constitutional rights based on changing times and circumstances.

The second major school is often referred to as **living constitutionalism.** Supporters of this approach believe the Constitution is a "living document" that should be interpreted, in the words of Chief Justice Earl Warren, according to "the evolving standards of decency that mark the progress of a maturing society." Justices who adopt this philosophy (also called **loose constructionism**) may look beyond the text of the Constitution to interpret its meaning; they tend to favor a case-by-case "balancing of the interests" approach, weighing the degree to which a statute infringes on a fundamental right against the government's interest in passing it.

Because of these differences in philosophy and approach, judges often differ on how to interpret the law and resolve the cases before them. This is why appellate courts have an odd number of judges—nine on the Supreme Court. The interpretation of law and the specific ruling that a majority (or at least a plurality) of the judges can agree upon becomes the legally binding opinion of the court. Judges can also write a concurring opinion if they agree with the outcome of the case but have a different interpretation of the law, or a dissenting opinion if they disagree with the outcome itself.

a.k.a. Loose Constructionism

Armed with this basic understanding of the common law, Supreme Court procedure, and the differing schools of constitutional interpretation, we are now ready to take on the First Amendment.

The best way to understand Supreme Court decisions is by being an active reader. Think to yourself as you go along: Is the Court making the right call here? What parts do you agree with, what parts do you disagree with, and why? To paraphrase a law school professor of mine, don't just look at what the justices are saying, look at what they are *doing*. Crafty legal minds are at work! The justices are more than just neutral arbiters of the law. They all have strong views on how the Constitution should be interpreted and write their opinions looking to shift the direction of the law for years, decades, or even centuries down the line. If this all sounds rather strange or confusing, don't worry. Read on!

Don't just look at what judges are SAYING, but what they are DOING !!!

# RELIGION:
# THE ESTABLISHMENT
# AND FREE EXERCISE
# CLAUSES

# ✦ 3 ✦

## WE'RE GONNA BUILD
## A BIG, BEAUTIFUL WALL . . .
## BETWEEN CHURCH AND STATE!

**A**MERICAN SOCIETY HAS ALWAYS HAD A COMPLICATED
relationship with religion. Contrary to the platitude that
America welcomes people of all faiths, history paints a far
less rosy picture. The fabled "City upon a Hill" of the New England
Puritans was a strict theocracy that banished religious dissenters like
Anne Hutchinson and Roger Williams for holding contrary views.

Quakers and Catholics were persecuted throughout the colonies, and Anglican Virginia in 1771 jailed fifty Baptists for preaching doctrines contrary to the *Book of Common Prayer*. It goes without saying that non-Christians were entirely unwelcome. Nor did the situation change following independence. While some states, such as Virginia, disestablished their churches, others continued to give official sanction to one religious denomination over all others.

The famous "wall of separation" between church and state appears nowhere in the U.S. Constitution. Rather, the idea comes from letters exchanged between President Thomas Jefferson and a congregation of Baptists in Danbury, Connecticut, in 1801–02. The Baptists wrote to the president complaining that Connecticut had established Congregationalism as the official state church and did not guarantee religious freedom to members of other denominations. Jefferson responded by affirming his belief that "religion is a matter which lies solely between man and his God," and that "the legislative powers of government reach actions only, and not opinions."

Then he took it a step further:

> *I contemplate with sovereign reverence that act of the whole American people which declared that their legislature would "make no law respecting an establishment of religion, or prohibiting the free exercise thereof" [i.e., the First Amendment], thus building a wall of separation between Church & State.*

While historians have long debated whether Jefferson's views on the meaning of the religion clauses were widely shared by delegates to the Constitutional Convention (which Jefferson did not attend, since he was in France), its impact on constitutional law is clear. His letter to the Danbury Baptists made its first Supreme Court appearance in the case of *Reynolds v. United States* (1878). Here, a Mormon polygamist named Reynolds had been convicted under a federal law that made it a crime to have more than one spouse. Reynolds challenged the conviction, claiming that the law unconstitutionally deprived him of the right to free exercise of his religion. The Supreme Court cited Jefferson's letter in its decision:

*Coming as this does from an acknowledged leader of the advocates of the [First Amendment], it may be accepted almost as an authoritative declaration of the scope and effect of the amendment.*

Even though they ruled against Reynolds and held that polygamy was not protected under the First Amendment (more about this later), Jefferson's interpretation of the First Amendment's religion clauses was now firmly cemented in Supreme Court jurisprudence.

As is often the case with the First Amendment, a little clarity in one area often raises new questions in others. Jefferson's "wall of separation" sounds nice in principle, but it's not always easy to apply in practice.

For instance, can the government provide financial assistance to a religion without "establishing" it? What if a religious organization is involved in carrying out a public function like running a school or hospital—can the government lend its support then? Does the Establishment Clause mandate that the state must be completely secular, or only that it cannot favor one religion over another?

And what about the Free Exercise Clause? Does "exercise" include freedom of religious practice or only freedom of religious belief? The

underlying issue behind all of these questions is just how thick a wall the First Amendment requires and whether a degree of permeability is acceptable in some areas.

# ✦ 4 ✦

## SUPPORTING RELIGIOUS SCHOOLS:
## WHEN THE COURT GIVES YOU THE LEMON TEST
## MAKE LEGAL LEMONADE

S OME THINGS UNDER THE ESTABLISHMENT CLAUSE
are quite clear. If the National Cathedral in Washington,
DC, were to fall on hard times, for example, Congress
could not appropriate a dime of taxpayer money to help it out. But
First Amendment issues are rarely this simple. For both sides, the primary battleground in the fight over church-state separation lies in the
domain of government support for parochial schools. Nearly all such
cases to reach the Supreme Court have had to do with public busing,
direct teaching subsidies, and voucher programs used to benefit religiously affiliated private schools.

The Supreme Court did not address the question of whether the Establishment Clause even applies to the states until *Everson v. Board of Education* (1947). This case involved a challenge to a New Jersey program that reimbursed parents who sent their children to parochial schools on public buses. Justice Hugo Black, writing the 5–4 opinion of the Court, settled the question definitively:

*The "establishment of religion" clause of the First Amendment means at least this: Neither a state nor the federal government can set up a church[,] . . . pass laws which aid one religion, aid all religions, or prefer one religion over another[,] . . . force nor influence a person to go to or to remain away from church against his will or force him to profess a belief or disbelief in any religion. . . . No tax in any amount, large or small, can be levied to support any religious activities or institutions . . . [or] to teach or practice religion. Neither a state nor the Federal Government can, openly or secretly, participate in the affairs of any religious organization or groups and vice versa. In the words of Jefferson, the clause against establishment of religious by law was intended to erect "a wall of separation between church and State."*

In spite of this seemingly absolutist language, the Court still ruled in favor of New Jersey, finding that the reimbursement policy furthered a legitimate educational function that was "separate and indisputably marked off from the religious function" of the schools. Justice Black ended his majority opinion with a clear declaration of how the Supreme Court would interpret Establishment Clause cases in the future:

*The First Amendment has erected a wall between church and state. That wall must be kept high and impregnable. We could not approve the slightest breach.*

The four justices who did not join Justice Black dissented because they believed the majority opinion did not go far enough in separating church and state. To the dissenters, the New Jersey program also ran afoul of the Establishment Clause because,

*The Amendment's purpose was [to] create a complete and permanent separation of the spheres of religious activity and civil authority by comprehensively forbidding every form of public aid or support for religion. . . . [T]he prohibition is absolute. . . .*

*Everson* is a great starting point for looking at how the Supreme Court operates in practice. All nine justices agreed that the Establishment Clause of the First Amendment is incorporated to the states and that Thomas Jefferson's "wall of separation between Church and State" is the right way to interpret its meaning. But how would this work in future cases? Even though the majority and dissenting justices shared essentially the same interpretation of the Constitution, they arrived at different conclusions when it came to applying the law to the facts.

It would be another twenty years before the Supreme Court took up another case dealing with government aid to religious schools. In *Board of Education v. Allen* (1968), a 6–3 majority held that it was not a violation of the Establishment Clause for a state to lend books on secular subjects to parochial schools. For all the tough talk about the "impregnable" wall separating church and state, the Court twice now had approved laws using public money to subsidize religious schools.

The landmark decision of *Lemon v. Kurtzman* (1971) finally brought some higher logic to Establishment Clause cases. *Lemon* concerned a Pennsylvania law that reimbursed teacher salaries at parochial schools from the state treasury. The majority in *Everson* had grudgingly conceded that public transportation reimbursements for students attending parochial schools were "within the State's constitutional power even though it approaches the verge of that power," but, they said, a direct subsidy to parochial school teachers went too far. In the *Lemon* case, the Court struck down the Pennsylvania statute and went a step further: it created a comprehensive formula that would apply in all future Establishment Clause cases.

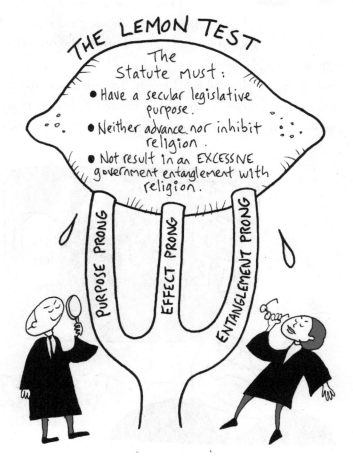

THE LEMON TEST

The Statute must:

- Have a secular legislative purpose.
- Neither advance nor inhibit religion.
- Not result in an EXCESSIVE government entanglement with religion.

PURPOSE PRONG

EFFECT PRONG

ENTANGLEMENT PRONG

Alton Lemon

1ST AMENDMENT HERO

The Lemon Test is one of the clearest articulations of Supreme Court thinking on a constitutional issue and a bête noire to originalist judges, who have been trying to overrule it for more than four decades. Justice Antonin Scalia, never one to sugarcoat things, vented the frustrations of originalists everywhere by describing the Lemon Test as "some ghoul in a late-night horror movie that repeatedly sits up in its grave and shuffles abroad, after being repeatedly killed and buried."

What, then, is this fabled Lemon Test? It's actually far less effervescent than it sounds. The Court created a three-part series of questions—called "prongs" in legalese—designed to probe the statute

THE LEMON TEST

Lemon Test

Antonin Scalia

— This Lemon Test leaves a sour taste.

and see if it passes constitutional muster. The first prong, or "purpose prong," requires the statute to have a "secular legislative purpose." This means that the reason or intent behind the statute must be to advance some nonreligious government objective. The second prong, or "effect prong," requires that "the principal or primary effect [of the statute] must be one that neither advances nor inhibits religion." This means that the statute's primary outcome must neither help nor harm religion. The third prong, or "entanglement prong," forbids the statute from "foster[ing] an excessive government entanglement with religion."

As you can see, there are no hard and fast rules here. The Lemon Test requires a careful examination of the facts in each case, balancing the particular interests involved. In *Lemon v. Kurtzman,* the Supreme Court struck down the Pennsylvania statute for violating the third prong since nearly all of the payments went to Catholic school teachers.

The year 1983 marked a sea change in the history of Establishment Clause jurisprudence. Ever since *Everson* back in 1947, the Supreme Court had tended to scrutinize public funds going to religious institutions with a critical eye. The Lemon Test formalized this approach by putting the burden on the government to prove that the statute was nonreligious in nature. Originalist judges never accepted this approach and argued that the text of the Constitution says nothing about a strict separation between church and state. Starting with the cases of *Mueller v. Allen* (1983) and *Marsh v. Chambers* (1983), the growing originalist faction on the high court began to fight back.

The Supreme Court in *Mueller* considered a challenge to a Minnesota statute that allowed taxpayers to deduct private educational expenses—including tuition payments to parochial schools—from their state income taxes. In a curious bit of signaling, the five-justice majority opinion, written by Justice William Rehnquist, applied the Lemon Test with the caveat that it provides "'no more than [a]

helpful signpost' in dealing with Establishment Clause challenges." The majority found that the statute passed the Lemon Test because it applied equally to parents who sent their children to religiously affiliated and non-religiously affiliated parochial schools. This "private choice" component would become a major element in future Establishment Clause cases.

*Marsh v. Chambers,* decided only a week after *Mueller,* addressed the question of whether the Establishment Clause forbids the government from paying state-supported chaplains. A Nebraska state senator challenged his state's hiring of an official chaplain to open legislative sessions with a prayer as a violation of the Establishment Clause. Both the federal District Court and the Circuit Court dutifully applied the Lemon Test, concluded that direct public funding of clergymen violates all three prongs, and declared such funding to be unconstitutional. The Supreme Court disagreed.

The majority opinion was a masterstroke of originalism. Since the United States had a history of state-supported chaplains going back to colonial days and since the First Congress had paid official chaplains, Rehnquist wrote, "clearly the men who wrote the First Amendment Religion Clauses did not view paid legislative chaplains and opening prayers as a violation of that Amendment." If the authors of the Establishment Clause didn't think that official chaplains were a problem, why should they bother a court sitting 200 years later? So the majority simply approved the statute without going through the motions of applying the Lemon Test.

What the *Mueller* and *Marsh* cases show is that the Lemon Test is more discretionary than mandatory and that the wall of separation between church and state is far from impermeable. The *Marsh* decision also revealed the growing influence of originalist thinking on the Supreme Court. The majority was not concerned with following *stare decisis* or looking to the standards of the time to resolve the case. Instead, it looked to the actions of the Founders in order to discern the "true meaning" of the Establishment Clause.

There is perhaps no better example of the shift that had occurred by the end of the 20th century than the case of *Agostini v. Felton* (1997). In the 1985 case of *Aguilar v. Felton*, the Supreme Court had struck down a New York City program that sent public school teachers to parochial schools in order to provide remedial education to disadvantaged children. Given the shifting attitudes on the Supreme Court over the succeeding twelve years, a group of petitioners saw their chance to have *Aguilar* overruled. Their gamble paid off. Even though the facts of *Aguilar* and *Agostini* were nearly identical, a 5–4 majority overruled the prior holding, noting that "*stare decisis* does not prevent us from overruling a previous decision where there has been a significant change in or subsequent development of our constitutional law." The majority also unveiled a new, more permissive interpretation of the Lemon Test. Now, a statute would be found permissible if it does not "result in governmental indoctrination; define its recipients by reference to religion; or create an excessive entanglement."

And the hits just kept on coming. Three years later, in *Mitchell v.*

*Helms* (2000), the Supreme Court overruled its decisions in *Meek v. Pittenger* (1975) and *Wolman v. Walter* (1977) that direct government lending of instructional materials such as maps, magazines, and electronic equipment to parochial schools failed the Lemon Test. *Stare decisis* went out the window again, as the justices voted 6–3 to uphold such lending and overruled *Meek* and *Wolman*. Justice Clarence Thomas, writing for a four-justice plurality, wanted to take it a step further and allow all government aid to religious schools as long as it is given on a "neutral" basis and not designed to promote religious indoctrination. Justice Sandra Day O'Connor—who became the first woman to sit on the high court in 1981—and Justice Steven Breyer agreed with the outcome but objected to the plurality's proposed rule as being "of unprecedented breadth." The three dissenting justices slammed the decision, stating: "The plurality would break the law. The majority misapplies it."

*Agostini* and *Mitchell* sent a clear signal that at least five of the justices favored allowing way more involvement between church and state than the Court in *Everson* ever could have dreamed of. The dispute over parochial school voucher programs removed any doubt. By the late 1990s, several states had begun experimenting with voucher programs that provided money to parents who wanted to take their children out of public schools and put them in private schools. Ohio was one of those states, implementing a voucher program for the Cleveland City School District. Of the 3,700 students who participated in that program for the 1999–2000 school year, over 96% enrolled in religiously affiliated private schools.

The Ohio program was challenged for violating the Establishment Clause, and the Supreme Court heard the appeal in *Zelman v. Simmons-Harris* (2002). In yet another 5–4 decision, the justices ruled in favor of the government, holding that voucher programs do not violate the First Amendment. The majority decision rested heavily on a finding of religious "neutrality" and "private choice" criteria; it did not even cite *Lemon v. Kurtzman* as authority, let alone apply the Lemon Test. While the Court did not explicitly overrule *Lemon*, it was clearly applying a different test regarding government aid programs: If the program is

*neutral with respect to religion, and provides assistance directly to a broad class of citizens who, in turn, direct government aid to religious schools wholly as a result of their own genuine and independent private choice, the program is not readily subject to challenge under the Establishment Clause.*

Once again, Justice Thomas thought the majority did not go far enough and wrote separately to call into question the very applicability of the Establishment Clause to the states. The four dissenters fired back, with Justice John Paul Stevens pointing out how far the *Zelman* decision strayed from prior precedents: "The Court has never in so many words . . . overruled *Everson*. [But how can] a Court consistently leave *Everson* on the books and approve the Ohio vouchers? The answer is that it cannot."

After more than seventy years, *Everson* lives on today in a weakened state; decades of Supreme Court decisions have whittled down its high wall of separation into little more than a speed bump. Similarly, *Lemon* is still technically good law, but it has been marginalized in favor of newer tests that are far more permissive of church-state intermingling. We will see a similar pattern play out as we move into issues pertaining to religion in public schools.

# ◆ 5 ◆

## GO TO THE PRINCIPAL'S OFFICE, AMEN:
## RELIGION IN PUBLIC SCHOOLS

J UST AS TOUCHY AS THE QUESTION OF GOVERNMENT
aid to parochial schools is whether the First Amendment
allows any intermingling of religion and public schools. The
Supreme Court first waded into the debate just one year after *Everson*, in
the case of *McCollum v. Board of Education* (1948). Here, the Court struck
down an Illinois program that set aside class time in public schools for
religious instruction by parochial teachers. Such a program, the justices found, subjected students to indoctrination through use of "the
state's compulsory public school machinery."

Four years later, however, a 6-3 majority in *Zorach v. Clauson* (1952)
upheld a New York program that permitted public schools to release
students from class in order to attend private religious instruction.
Why the difference? In *Zorach*, the majority held that offering religious

instruction on public property could be interpreted as an official endorsement of that religious belief, while allowing students to leave class to attend religious instruction was merely an accommodation to religious belief. The majority opinion, written by Justice William O. Douglas, declared:

*[W]e are a religious people whose institutions presuppose a Supreme Being. . . . When the state encourages religious instruction or cooperates with religious authorities by adjusting the schedule of public events to sectarian needs, it follows the best of our traditions.*

Justice Jackson, writing in dissent, noted the divergence of this language from the separationism in *Everson:* "[T]he wall which the Court was professing to erect between Church and State has become even more warped and twisted than I expected."

The next time the Supreme Court took up religion in a public school case was a decade later in *Engel v. Vitale* (1962). The New York Board of Regents had authorized an official prayer to be recited before the beginning of the school day that read: "Almighty God, we acknowledge our dependence upon Thee, and we beg Thy blessings upon us, our parents, our teachers, and our Country. Amen." A group of parents challenged the prayer for violating the First Amendment; the U.S. Supreme Court took the appeal after New York's highest court affirmed the prayer as constitutional.

A six-justice majority of the Supreme Court voted to overturn the New York decision and struck down the prayer. The Establishment Clause, they argued,

> *must at least mean that . . . it is no part of the business of government to compose official prayers for any group of American people to recite as a part of a religious program carried on by government.*

A year later, in *Abington School District v. Schempp* (1963), the Supreme Court likewise declared that Bible reading in public schools violates the Establishment Clause.

With the broad scope of the *Engel* and *Abington* rulings, it would be more than twenty years before another school prayer case came before the Supreme Court. The question in the 1985 case of *Wallace v. Jaffree* was whether an Alabama statute that set aside one minute at the start of each day for meditation "or voluntary prayer" was constitutionally permissible. The Court held that it was not, voting 6–3 that the practice failed the first prong of the Lemon Test by lacking a secular purpose.

The *Wallace* decision at first seems unremarkable. The Supreme Court had been clear in both *Engel* and *Abington* that it viewed religion in public schools with a high degree of skepticism; this decision appears to follow in those footsteps. Looking back, the part of *Wallace* that really stands out is a blistering dissent by Justice Rehnquist, hinting at the new direction the Supreme Court would take when he became chief justice the following year.

Rehnquist began by launching an all-out attack on the very idea that Jefferson's "wall of separation" is an authoritative interpretation of the Establishment Clause. The dissent reads more like a history paper than a legal opinion, as Justice Rehnquist goes through the writings of Jefferson, Madison, and the other Founders to make his case. After a lengthy discussion of the 1789 *Congressional Record* and various instances of government aid to churches in the early republic, Justice Rehnquist concluded that the First Amendment "did not require government neutrality between religion and irreligion, nor did it prohibit the Federal Government from providing nondiscriminatory aid to religion." There was, he went on, "simply no historical foundation for the proposition that the Framers intended to build the 'wall of separation' that was constitutionalized in *Everson*." Since the wall of separation was merely a "metaphor based on bad history" and had proven to be "useless as a guide to judging," Rehnquist urged that it "should be frankly and explicitly abandoned." In his view, the determining factor in the interpretation of the Constitution should be the intent of the Framers, not the whims of judges in trying to interpret contemporary social values.

William Rehnquist became chief justice of the United States in 1986 and was joined that same year by new associate justice and ardent originalist, Antonin Scalia. Clarence Thomas, perhaps the most doctrinaire originalist on the Court, won his seat after a legendarily contentious confirmation battle in 1991. Meanwhile, the Court lost its two strongest proponents of Living Constitutionalism: Justices Thurgood Marshall and William Brennan.

The first religion in public school case to come before the Rehnquist Court was *Lee v. Weisman* (1992). Court watchers everywhere wondered: Would it overturn a half-century of precedent and roll back *Everson*? Would *Lemon* be on the chopping block? Would the wall of separation still stand, or would the justices dismantle the legal barriers dividing church and state?

*Lee* challenged the practice of a Rhode Island middle school of inviting a priest, minister, or rabbi to deliver a nonsectarian prayer at its graduation ceremony. In a surprise ending, a 5–4 majority of the Supreme Court ruled against the school district and found that even a nondenominational prayer delivered by a member of the clergy violates the Establishment Clause. Justice Anthony Kennedy, a new appointee following the failed 1987 nomination of hardline originalist Robert Bork, proved to be the crucial swing vote (a position he would hold for his entire career). Kennedy eschewed the Lemon Test in favor of a new "coercion test" of his own creation. According to this formulation, "at a minimum, the Constitution guarantees that government may not coerce anyone to support or participate in religion or its exercise." No other justice signed on to Kennedy's test, but four did agree that the prayers violate the Establishment Clause. Unsurprisingly, the four originalist judges all dissented.

The last school prayer case to come before the Supreme Court was *Santa Fe Independent School District v. Doe* (2000). The issue here was the policy of a Texas high school that allowed students to elect a class chaplain who would deliver prayers over the public address system prior to home football games. The justices ruled 6–3 that the policy was unconstitutional since it was functionally similar to the graduation prayers in *Lee.* The fact that the prayers were student-led did not make them private student speech because: "[t]hese invocations are authorized by a government policy and take place on government property at government-sponsored school-related events." According to the three dissenting justices, the majority decision "bristles with hostility to all things religious in public life," but the precedent was clear: Because children are legally required to attend school and their impressionable age makes them susceptible to coercion from teachers and peer pressure from other students, the Supreme Court will view almost any official entanglement between public schools and religion as impermissible.

Another area where religion and public education intersect is the curriculum. The teaching of evolution has been a minefield in the United States for nearly a century. The issue first became famous with the "Scopes Monkey Trial" of 1925, when Tennessee prosecuted high school science teacher John Scopes for illegally teaching evolution in a public school. The U.S. Supreme Court didn't take up the question until *Epperson v. Arkansas* in 1968. Arkansas had passed a law similar to Tennessee's, criminalizing the teaching of evolution in public schools. All nine high court justices voted in favor of striking down the law, declaring that states may not require "that teaching and learning . . . be tailored to the principles or prohibitions of any religious sect or dogma."

While states could not prohibit the teaching of evolution, *Epperson* did not address the question of whether teaching creationism is permissible. In the following decades, a number of states mandated that biology courses include lessons in "creation science" alongside the theory of evolution in order to "teach the controversy." A challenge to one such mandate came before the U.S. Supreme Court in the case of *Edwards v. Aguillard* (1987).

Louisiana forbade the teaching of evolution unless the instructor also devoted equal time to teaching "creation science." Justice Brennan, writing the opinion of the Court, called the stated purpose of the law—to "advance academic freedom . . . [by] teaching all of the evidence"—a "sham." Rather, he said, "[t]he preeminent purpose of the Louisiana legislature was clearly to advance the religious viewpoint that a supernatural being created humankind." Thus, because it failed the first prong of the Lemon Test, the Court struck down the Louisiana law and, by implication, rendered invalid all similar state laws requiring instruction in creationism. Justices Scalia and Rehnquist, writing in dissent, again argued that the Lemon Test should be abandoned for having "no basis in the language or history of the [First] Amendment."

Although *Edwards* is the most recent evolution case to come before the Supreme Court, it has a postscript. A "creation science" textbook industry had begun to develop in the early 1980s and was ready to make a nationwide push if the Supreme Court ruled in favor of Louisiana in *Edwards*. When this didn't happen, creationists latched on to a passage at the end of the majority opinion that provided a possible loophole: "[T]eaching a variety of scientific theories about the origins of humankind to schoolchildren might be validly done with the clear secular intent of enhancing the effectiveness of science instruction." A book entitled *Of Pandas and People* was published in 1989 that presented creationism as a legitimate science, giving it the label "intelligent design theory," or ID.

Fast-forward to 2004. A Pennsylvania school district has decided to change the biology curriculum to include the teaching of intelligent design, using *Of Pandas and People* as a standard text. A group of parents challenges the decision in federal court, resulting in the case of *Kitzmiller, et al. v. Dover Area School District* (2005). In a 139-page decision issued that December, District Judge John Edward Jones III systemically examines the claims that ID is a legitimate science and dismisses them as "a pretext for the Board's real purpose, which was to promote religion in the public school classroom, in violation of the Establishment Clause." The school district did not appeal the decision, so the Supreme Court never had the opportunity to hear the case. While *Kitzmiller* is only a District Court decision and not binding precedent, its lengthy opinion and extensive legal reasoning has seemingly settled the question that teaching intelligent design in public schools violates the Establishment Clause.

# ◆ 6 ◆

## PUBLIC DISPLAY:
## YOUR CRÈCHE IS SHOWING

**T**HE FINAL AREA OF THE ESTABLISHMENT CLAUSE we will discuss is whether religious displays on government property violate the First Amendment. We can say definitively that displaying the Christian cross on top of a government building is out because that would constitute a clear endorsement of religion. But what about less obvious examples, like nativity scenes in public parks, menorahs in classrooms, or the Ten Commandments in a courthouse? Legal disputes over such issues are known as public display cases.

The Supreme Court did not take up a public display case until 1980 in *Stone v. Graham*. The issue in *Stone* was a Kentucky statute that required the Ten Commandments to be posted on the wall of every public school classroom, with the funding to come from private sources. An eight-justice majority applied the Lemon Test and struck down the law for lacking a secular legislative purpose. Justice William Rehnquist, the lone dissenter, argued that even though the Ten Commandments are a sacred text, they also "have had a significant impact on the development of secular legal codes of the Western World . . . and [have] been closely identified with our history and government." Once again, Rehnquist's dissent would find traction in later cases.

The Court took up another public display case only four years later in *Lynch v. Donnelly* (1984). Every holiday season, the city of Pawtucket, Rhode Island, had erected a Christmas display in a downtown park owned by a nonprofit organization. The display included a Santa Claus house, reindeer, candy cane poles, a Christmas tree, a banner that read "Seasons Greetings," and a crèche containing plastic statues of the baby Jesus, Mary, Joseph, and various angels, animals, and wise men. A group of residents challenged the crèche in federal court for violating the Establishment Clause. Both the District Court and Circuit Court agreed that it did; the Supreme Court, however, did not.

Chief Justice Warren Burger began the majority opinion by noting that there has been "an unbroken history of official acknowledgement by all three branches of government of the role of religion in American life from at least 1789." By way of example, he cited prayers by the Founding Fathers for divine guidance and thanksgiving, the designation of Christmas as a national holiday, the appearance of the motto "In God We Trust" on national currency, and the phrase "one Nation under God" in the Pledge of Allegiance. As opposed to the "high and impregnable" wall of separation declared in *Everson*, the majority in *Lynch* now characterized the wall between church and state as only a "metaphor"—and not a "wholly accurate" one at that. According to the majority opinion, it was neither "possible [nor] desirable to enforce a regime of total separation," and the "Constitution [does not] require complete separation of church and state." Instead, the ruling went on, the Constitution

> *affirmatively mandates accommodation, not merely tolerance, of all religions, and forbids hostility toward any.*

The Founders' intent in creating the Establishment Clause, Burger wrote, had been to forbid the creation of an official church of the United States, but that is "of far less concern today. . . . Any notion that these symbols pose a real danger of establishment of a state church is farfetched indeed."

Hey, c'mon. There's always been some religion in our history.

The Founders just didn't want an established 'church of the United States', that's all.

Warren Burger

The four dissenting justices applied the Lemon Test and concluded that a publicly supported nativity scene fails all three prongs. They again criticized the majority opinion for ignoring *Lemon*, which the majority quite clearly had done. Justice Brennan acknowledged that not all invocations of God necessarily violate the Establishment Clause—the national motto and pledge of allegiance are examples of what he called "ceremonial deism"—but criticized the majority opinion as "a long step backwards to the days when Justice Brewer could arrogantly declare for the Court that 'this is a Christian nation.'"

Justice Harry Blackmun, in a separate dissent, regarded the Pawtucket victory as "Pyrrhic," because the crèche would now be displayed in a setting where "Christians feel constrained in acknowledging its symbolic meaning and non-Christians feel alienated by its presence. Surely, this is a misuse of a sacred symbol."

Perhaps the most important piece of the fractured decision in *Lynch* was the sole concurring opinion by Justice Sandra Day O'Connor. She agreed with the majority decision but proposed a new method for analyzing Establishment Clauses cases. For her, the primary purpose of the Establishment Clause is to "prohibit government from making adherence to a religion relevant in any way to a person's standing in the political community," especially by endorsing a particular religion. This, she maintained, "sends a message to nonadherents that they are outsiders, not full members of the political community." Justice O'Connor did not propose that *Lemon* should be overruled; instead, she argued that her "endorsement test" would help clarify what courts should be analyzing when they look at its purpose and effect prongs. Simple "acknowledgments" of religion, such as the national motto, the Pledge of Allegiance, or displays of the crèche are fine, in Justice O'Connor's view; only an outright endorsement of religion crosses the constitutional line.

Just when they thought the crèche was out, the Supreme Court pulled it back in five years later in *Allegheny County v. American Civil Liberties Union* (1989). The outcome was incredibly messy, reflecting the extreme divisions on the Court, as six different justices ended up writing their own opinions. The facts of the case were strikingly similar to those in *Lynch*. At issue were two religious displays on public property in the city of Pittsburgh. The first was a crèche located on the main staircase of a county courthouse, with an angel carrying a banner that read "Gloria in Excelsis Deo!" ("Glory to God in the Highest!"); the other display was a menorah placed next to a Christmas tree located in front of the city hall with a sign reading: "Salute to Liberty."

The most important takeaway from the case is the fact that five justices agreed to adopt Justice O'Connor's endorsement test as part of their analysis, including Justices Brennan and Marshall, who up to this point had been Lemon Test absolutists. Applying the endorsement test, the five justices found the free-standing crèche display to be unconstitutional because, "here, unlike in *Lynch,* nothing in the context of the display detracts from the crèche's religious message."

The four dissenters, Justices Kennedy, Rehnquist, White, and Scalia, explicitly rejected the endorsement test for displaying "an unjustified hostility towards religion." Instead, they proposed a narrower "coercion test," whereby the "government may not coerce anyone to support or participate in any religion or its exercise"; it "may not . . . give direct benefits to religion," but it should permit "flexible accommodation or passive acknowledgement of existing symbols . . . that are accepted in our national heritage" such as the crèche and menorah.

69

OK. What we need is a 'Coercion Test'. Let's make it that the State can't give direct benefits to religion, but can accommodate traditional symbols.

The dissenters could claim a partial victory because Justices O'Connor and Blackmun sided with them in upholding the menorah display. Although they applied different tests, six justices concluded that the menorah was permissible because it stood next to a Christmas tree, and the sign saluting liberty made it "not exclusively religious"—part of an "overall holiday setting" where both Christmas and Hanukkah were being celebrated as secular holidays. Justices Brennan, Marshall, and Stevens would have forbidden the menorah as well, taking a strict separationist approach: "[T]he Establishment Clause should be construed to create a strong presumption against the display of religious symbols on public property."

Perhaps because the nine justices couldn't agree on a single test, the Supreme Court held off on taking another public display case for more than a decade. Their next crack at it came sixteen years later in the twin cases of *McCreary County v. American Civil Liberties Union* (2005) and *Van Orden v. Perry* (2005). Despite dealing with nearly identical issues on the very same day, the Supreme Court somehow reached different conclusions in the two cases!

Let's start with *McCreary County*. Here the issue was a series of attempts by several Kentucky counties to place large placards of the Ten Commandments in their courthouses. The first was a freestanding display of the Ten Commandments. The ACLU challenged that display, and a federal court struck it down. On the second attempt, instead of hanging the Ten Commandments alone, the county included such other documents as the Magna Carta, Mayflower Compact, Declaration of Independence, and Bill of Rights, showing how certain parts reflect the religious heritage of American law. This, too, was struck down in federal court. In the final attempt, the Ten Commandments was displayed with the other documents but without highlighting the religion issue. This was what the Supreme Court had to decide on in *McCreary County*.

The majority refused the counties' request to examine the third attempt in isolation, since "the world is not made brand new every morning . . . [T]he Counties' position just bucks common sense: reasonable observers have reasonable memories, and our precedents sensibly forbid an observer to turn a blind eye to the context in which [the] policy arose." Taking a holistic view of the facts, the majority engaged in an old-fashioned Lemon Test analysis and struck down the displays on the grounds that their purpose was religious in nature.

Justice Scalia wrote an aggressive dissent, joined by Justices Thomas, Rehnquist, and Kennedy, that attacked *Lemon*, Living Constitutionalism, and the entire wall of separation theory. According to Justice Scalia, "the Court's oft repeated assertion that the government cannot favor religious practice . . . [is] demonstrably false." By way of argument, he maintained, "The Establishment Clause permits [the] disregard of polytheists and believers in unconcerned deities, just as it permits the disregard of devout atheists." Justice Scalia then turned his guns on Justice Stevens's view that the Court should examine "the meaning of constitutional provisions with one eye towards our Nation's history and the other fixed on its democratic aspirations" as lacking "consistently applied principle." In other words, *Lemon* is the fruit of Living Constitutionalism (pardon the pun) and "since its inception . . . [has] been manipulated to fit whatever result the Court aimed to achieve."

Justice O'Connor wrote a characteristically pragmatic concurrence, attempting to bridge the chasm between the two sides by pointing out: "Reasonable minds can disagree about how to apply the Religion Clauses in a given case. But the goal of the Clauses is clear: to carry out the Founders' plan of preserving religious liberty to the fullest extent possible in a pluralistic society." That said, O'Connor outright rejects the dissent's claim that the First Amendment protects only the Abrahamic religions:

> We [cannot] accept the theory that Americans who do not accept the Commandments' validity are outside the First Amendment's protections. . . . It is true that the Framers lived at a time when our national religious diversity was neither as robust nor as well recognized as it is now . . . [b]ut they did know that line-drawing between religions is an enterprise that, once begun, has no logical stopping point. . . . Those who would renegotiate the boundaries between church and state must therefore answer a difficult question: Why would we trade a system that has served us so well for one that has served others so poorly?

Mere hours after striking down the display of the Ten Commandments in *McCreary County,* the Supreme Court affirmed a similar display in the Texas state capitol in *Van Orden v. Perry*—demonstrating again the bitter divisions between the justices. The only difference between the two cases was that Justice Steven Breyer switched his vote in *Van Orden* because he felt that the Texas display satisfied the secular purpose prong of *Lemon.* The difference for him was that the display had been donated by a private organization and sat alongside dozens of other monuments reflecting the "historical ideals" of Texas.

It's slightly surreal to see nearly every justice citing *McCreary County* as support for their decision in *Van Orden* as if it was a time-honored precedent rather than a ruling they had issued just before lunch. The main difference was that the four dissenters from *McCreary County* formed the plurality in *Van Orden.* They decided the case without using the Lemon Test but were not able to get a fifth vote to overrule it. And so, Chief Justice Rehnquist wrote for the majority, "Whatever may be the fate of the Lemon Test in the larger scheme of Establishment Clause jurisprudence, we think it not useful in dealing with the sort of passive monument that Texas has erected on its Capitol grounds."

An exasperated Justice Stevens issued a lengthy dissent that was in many ways the Living Constitutionalist rebuttal to Scalia's originalist manifesto from *McCreary County*. He began by rejecting Scalia's approach as one that "would eviscerate the heart of the Establishment Clause . . . replac[ing] Jefferson's 'wall of separation' with a perverse wall of exclusion." Instead, Stevens maintained, the Court's duty was to interpret the text "not by merely asking what those words meant to observers at the time of the founding, but instead by deriving from the Clause's text and history the broad principles that remain valid today."

The justices had agreed to hear two such similar appeals in the same term because they expected to deliver a clear, comprehensive decision on public display cases. What they ended up with was the exact opposite—a mess of separate opinions full of blatantly personal attacks that somehow managed to produce different outcomes in two nearly identical cases. It has been well over a decade since *McCreary County* and *Van Orden* were decided, and the Supreme Court still has not reached a consensus on how to analyze public display cases. The case of *Salazar v. Buono* (2010), challenging a cross erected in California's Mojave National Preserve by the Veterans of Foreign Wars in the 1930s, had the potential to be a landmark decision, but once again the Court fractured into six separate, disjointed opinions that allowed the cross to remain standing by a three-justice plurality decision.

The Supreme Court's inability to articulate a single standard means that local governments and lower courts have little guidance as to when religious symbols on public property cross the line from mere "acknowledgement" into unconstitutional "endorsement." The justices treat public display cases like a game of Calvinball, with each making up his or her own rules as they go along. Given the ongoing ideological divisions on the Court, the chances of this situation changing any time soon appear to be unlikely.

# ✦ 7 ✦

## FIGURING OUT THE FREE EXERCISE CLAUSE: IS IT PEYOTE BEFORE POLYGAMY, OR CONTRACEPTION COVERAGE BEFORE SANTERÍA?

THE FREE EXERCISE CLAUSE IS ALMOST LIKE A bridge that links the religious protections of the Establishment Clause to the speech and association protections in the rest of the First Amendment. It simultaneously prohibits the government from discriminating against certain religious beliefs while granting individuals the right to exercise their faith however they see fit. By now your finely tuned analytical antennae are probably standing on end. What exactly does the "exercise" of religion mean, and how far should its protections extend?

Let's start with the easy parts and move on from there. We can say definitively that the Free Exercise Clause guarantees all forms of personal religious belief. The government can never ban a religion. Period. But while freedom of belief is absolute, freedom of practice is not.

Freedom of belief is ABSOLUTE.

But freedom of PRACTICE? Well, that depends.

More than any other part of the Constitution, the Free Exercise Clause potentially allows individuals to "opt out" of laws that restrict their ability to act on their beliefs. The tension between allowing for the free and open practice of all religions in a diverse society, while at the same time not allowing every individual to exercise a personal religious veto over laws they don't like, forms the crux of the Supreme Court's Free Exercise Clause jurisprudence.

The first Free Exercise Clause case the Supreme Court took up was *Reynolds v. United States* (1878), the Mormon polygamy case discussed in Chapter 3. The Morrill Anti-Bigamy Act, a federal law criminalizing the practice of polygamy in the national territories, was passed by wide margins in both the House and Senate in 1862, and swiftly signed into law by President Abraham Lincoln. Reynolds, who was convicted under the law, appealed to the Supreme Court and lost 9–0.

In the unanimous opinion of the justices, Congress has no "legislative power over mere opinion," but the Free Exercise Clause leaves it free to restrict practices "which were in violation of social duties or subversive of good order." Allowing citizens to ignore laws that violate their religious beliefs, the justices maintained, would make those beliefs "superior to the law of the land, and in effect to permit every citizen to become a law unto himself."

With this definitive ruling, no Free Exercise case came before the Supreme Court for another sixty years, until *Cantwell v. Connecticut* (1940). This one was important both because it incorporated the Free Exercise Clause to the states and because it expanded its protections beyond mere belief. *Cantwell* concerned a Connecticut statute that required people to obtain a license from the state if they wanted to proselytize their faith in public. Before granting the license, the state official would need to certify the "bona fide" nature of the religion and that it conformed to "reasonable standards of efficiency and integrity." Two Jehovah's Witnesses, who had refused to obtain the license on religious grounds, actively proselytized in a heavily Roman Catholic neighborhood of New Haven and were arrested for violating the statute after nearly causing a riot.

A unanimous Supreme Court ruled in favor of the Jehovah's Witnesses and struck down the Connecticut statute for violating the Free Exercise Clause. The opinion began by reiterating the belief-action distinction from *Reynolds*, but declared that the government may not "condition the solicitation of aid for the perpetuation of religious views or systems upon a license, the grant of which rests in the exercise of a determination by state authority as to what is a religious cause." In other words, while the government is free to legislate actions, it cannot factor religious beliefs into its decision making.

The next landmark Free Exercise Clause case to come before the high court was *Sherbert v. Verner* in 1963. The appellant was a Seventh-day Adventist who had been fired from her job for refusing to work on Saturdays. When she applied for state unemployment benefits, South Carolina denied her claim because she refused to take any jobs that required Saturday work. For the first time, a majority of the Supreme Court applied strict scrutiny in a Free Exercise Clause case. (Quick refresher: strict scrutiny means that the burden is on the government to prove that the law is absolutely necessary to further a compelling state interest—a very high bar.) Applying the new and deliciously named Sherbert Test, seven justices voted to overrule the denial of unemployment benefits for violating the Free Exercise Clause, finding that South Carolina's interest in reducing unemployment fraud was not sufficiently compelling. Even if it was, they held, there were other ways the state could have furthered that interest that did not infringe on the right to free exercise.

The expansive protections recognized by the Court in *Sherbert* paved the way for a slew of other Free Exercise Clause challenges in the 1970s. The most consequential decision of this period was *Wisconsin v. Yoder* (1972). Yoder, a member of the Old Order Amish, was fined for refusing to send his daughter to school until the age of sixteen, in violation of Wisconsin law. Applying the Sherbert Test, the Supreme Court overturned the fine for violating the Free Exercise Clause. For the first time, the high court also rejected the binary belief-action distinction from *Reynolds* because "belief and action cannot be neatly confined in logic-tight compartments."

The Supreme Court rules that this cartoon violates the restriction of corny jokes in this book!

*Yoder* would turn out to be the high-water mark of the Sherbert Test, as the tide receded in the 1980s. In *United States v. Lee* (1982), the Supreme Court refused to extend the holding of *Yoder* to exempt the

Old Order Amish from the requirement to pay Social Security taxes. In this instance, the Court applied the strict scrutiny standard of the Sherbert Test (or at least paid lip service to it) and still ruled in favor of the government. The maintenance of a Social Security system, it held, was a compelling state interest and there was "no principled way" to carve out a religious tax exemption.

After *Lee*, the Supreme Court continued to reject Free Exercise Clause challenges. In *Bob Jones University v. United States* (1983), the justices ruled 8–0 that the IRS's denial of tax-exempt status to Bob Jones University for the school's racially discriminatory practices did not violate the Free Exercise Clause. Once again, while claiming to apply the strict-scrutiny Sherbert Test, the Court ruled in favor of the government on the grounds that its interest in eradicating racial discrimination in higher education was compelling and that the denial of tax-exempt status was necessary to further that goal.

After that, the Sherbert Test melted away faster than its namesake on a hot summer day.

In the 1986 case of *Goldman v. Weinberger*, a five-justice majority refused to apply the test at all when an Orthodox Jewish officer challenged the Air Force ban on wearing a yarmulke with his dress uniform. The justices held that "courts must give great deference" to the military in Free Exercise Clause cases and need not apply the same standards as they would to civilians. Likewise, the Court refused to apply the Sherbert Test in the case of *O'Lone v. Estate of Shabazz* (1987), rejecting a Free Exercise Clause challenge by Islamic inmates to prison work schedules that prevented them from attending religious services.

The Supreme Court decision in *Employment Division v. Smith* (1990) delivered the coup de grâce to the Sherbert Test. This was especially ironic because the facts of the case were so similar to those in *Sherbert*. The appellant was a member of a Native American Church who had been fired from his job for having ingested peyote as part of a religious ritual. When he applied for unemployment benefits, the State of Oregon denied his claim on the grounds that he was fired for "misconduct" (peyote use being a crime). In a 5–4 decision, a majority of the Supreme Court upheld Oregon's decision, declining to apply the Sherbert Test and returning to the old *Reynolds* belief-action distinction. Justice Scalia, writing for the majority, noted that the Sherbert Test was functionally a dead letter anyway, since the Court had ignored it so frequently, and that using strict scrutiny in Free Exercise cases was dangerous: "Any society adopting such a system would be courting anarchy . . . [allowing] religious exemptions from civil obligations of almost every conceivable kind."

But you can't fire me! This is part of my religious ritual.

And so, after more than a decade of weakening, watering down, and limiting the scope of the test, the Supreme Court decided that it would no longer apply strict scrutiny in Free Exercise Clause cases. But then something happened. In 1993, the pendulum began to swing back in the direction of Free Exercise claimants. First there was a favorable Supreme Court decision in the case of *Church of Lukumi Babalu Aye v. City of Hialeah*—the first time since *Wisconsin v. Yoder* that a challenger won a Free Exercise challenge involving something other than unemployment benefits.

*Church of Lukumi Babalu Aye* was rare in that it involved an overt government attempt to outlaw a religious practice. When a Santería church, whose practices involved the ritual slaughter and consumption of sacrificial animals, announced plans to open a worship center in Hialeah, Florida, the city council held an emergency public session in 1987 to keep out the church. The council passed a resolution noting the "concern" of many city residents about "certain religions [that] may propose to engage in practices which are inconsistent with public morals, peace or safety" and declaring "its commitment to a prohibition against any and all of [such] religious groups." Later in the year, the city council passed three ordinances that criminalized "sacrifices of animals for any type of ritual, regardless of whether or not the flesh or blood of the animal is to be consumed"—effectively banning a core part of Santería practice.

In a rare unanimous decision, all nine justices on the Supreme Court agreed that the city of Hialeah had violated the Free Exercise Clause by passing such an ordinance. Yet they could not agree on the reason why the ordinance should be invalidated. Justice Kennedy's majority opinion, joined in part by Justices Stevens, Breyer, Blackmun, and O'Connor, held that when a law is not neutral but rather designed "to infringe upon or restrict practices because of their religious motivation," then it must pass strict scrutiny in order to survive. Because the Hialeah ordinance was not neutral and its restrictions were overly broad, it failed strict scrutiny review. Justices Blackmun, Souter, and O'Connor wrote separately to argue that *Smith* had been wrongly decided and urged a reexamination of the Sherbert Test.

They didn't have to wait long. Later in 1993, Congress passed and President Bill Clinton signed into law the Religious Freedom Restoration Act (RFRA), mandating the use of the Sherbert Test in all Free

Exercise Clause cases. To say that this was unprecedented is an understatement! Legislatively mandating that the courts apply a particular legal test in certain types of cases touches on all kinds of separation of powers issues. Five years later, in *City of Boerne v. Flores* (1997), the Supreme Court struck down the portion of the RFRA as it applied to the states, but left its requirements intact for federal cases. As a result, two different standards are now used in Free Exercise Clause cases: the deferential *Smith* standard, used for challenges to actions taken by a state government that burden religious practice; and the restrictive *Sherbert* standard of the RFRA, used for actions taken by the federal government that burden religious practice.

All of which brings us to the landmark 2014 case of *Burwell v. Hobby Lobby*. Hobby Lobby was a privately owned, for-profit arts and crafts retailer with hundreds of stores throughout the United States that was founded by an Evangelical Christian whose stated purpose was to operate the company "in a manner consistent with Biblical principles." In 2010, Congress passed and President Barack Obama signed into law the Affordable Care Act, overhauling the nation's health-care system. One of the law's many provisions was a requirement that employers who hire over fifty people must provide their employees with health insurance policies that include coverage for contraceptive devices approved by the FDA. Hobby Lobby objected to providing coverage for forms of contraception that it considered abortifacients, such as morning-after pills and IUDs. The government allowed religious employers and nonprofit institutions to claim exemptions from the contraception mandate, but it did not make this option available to for-profit corporations. The penalty for failing to provide the coverage was $100 per employee per day, which in Hobby Lobby's case would have come out to $1.3 million per day, or about $475 million per year.

Hobby Lobby sued the Department of Health and Human Services to prevent enforcement of the penalty, claiming that the contraception mandate violated their religious beliefs. Since the actions of the federal government were being challenged, the heightened *Sherbert* standard of the RFRA would apply. The Supreme Court thus faced three big questions: First, since the RFRA protects "persons," could Hobby Lobby even bring a claim as a for-profit corporation? Second, even if Hobby Lobby is considered a person, could a corporation "exercise religion" under the RFRA? And finally, if Hobby Lobby can exercise religion, does the contraception mandate survive strict scrutiny analysis?

In a 5–4 decision, the Court ruled that corporations are considered people, that they can exercise religion under the RFRA, and that the contraception mandate failed strict scrutiny review. Justice Samuel Alito, writing the opinion of the Court, argued that the protections granted under the RFRA are broad enough to encompass "legal fictions" such as corporate entities, which are "simply a form of organization used by human beings to achieve desired ends." We will see the same reasoning used later when we discuss the famous *Citizens United* case.

Once it was found that Hobby Lobby could bring a claim under the RFRA, the rest was a fait accompli. The contraception mandate substantially burdened the company's exercise of religion, and it was not necessary to accomplish the compelling state interest in providing contraceptive coverage. "The most straightforward way of doing this," argued Justice Alito, "would be for the government to assume the cost of providing the [contraceptive coverage] to any women who are unable to obtain them under their health-insurance policies due to their employers' religious objections."

Justice Ruth Bader Ginsburg issued a fiery dissent, joined by Justices Sonia Sotomayor, Steven Breyer, and Elena Kagan, criticizing the majority decision for holding that "commercial enterprises, including corporations . . . can opt out of any law (saving only tax laws) they judge incompatible with their sincerely held religious beliefs." To the dissenters, the majority's proposed alternative of having "the government, i.e., the general public, pick up the tab" was no solution at all. Of most concern to the dissenters were the "untoward effects" the majority decision was bound to have. Despite the majority's attempt to limit the scope of their decision to closely held corporations, the dissenters had "[l]ittle doubt that RFRA claims will proliferate [and invite] for-profit entities to seek religion-based exemptions from regulations they deem offensive to their faith."

The Supreme Court has not taken up another Free Exercise case under the RFRA, so the potential reach of *Burwell v. Hobby Lobby* is still very much up in the air. It is entirely possible that the justices will limit its application to a narrow category of religiously based enterprises, as the majority seemed to imply; on the other hand, the dissent's fear of a slippery slope, in which for-profit corporations seek all manner of special exemptions and carve-outs, might also come true. Regardless of what happens, the implications of *Burwell* are huge. For the first time, the Supreme Court recognized the ability of a for-profit corporation to have constitutionally protected religious beliefs that exempt it from laws of general applicability.

It's important to look back and recognize what a departure this is from the concern in *Reynolds* that an expansive reading of the Free Exercise Clause would allow every citizen to become a "law unto himself." It also marks a trend in recent Supreme Court decisions that expands the concept of corporate personhood to encompass rights previously limited only to natural persons.

# EXPRESSION:
# FREEDOMS OF SPEECH,
# THE PRESS, ASSEMBLY,
# PETITION, AND
# ASSOCIATION

# ✦ 8 ✦

## SEDITIOUS LIBEL, BAD TENDENCIES, AND ALIEN PROVOCATEURS, OH MY!

**I**F YOU WERE TO ASK MOST AMERICANS: "WHAT'S THE first thing that comes to mind when I say First Amendment?" chances are that the vast majority would respond: "Free speech!"

The idea that all people should have an open forum to speak their minds, regardless of how distasteful or offensive their opinions might be, is a core principle of American democracy. The concept has also been embraced far beyond the borders of the United States, widely regarded as a basic human right and enshrined in the UN Universal Declaration of Rights. As we shall see, however, not all speech is absolutely free all of the time, and the idea that speech should be free at all is a relatively new concept, even in the context of American history.

The common law of England contained no freedom of speech protections. Seditious libel, a broad term that included bringing "hatred or contempt" upon the monarch, parliament, or church, was a criminal offense in both England and the colonies. Proof that the statement was true was no defense, and no defamatory intent was required; simply proving that the libelous statement had been intentionally published was enough to warrant a guilty verdict. Using the monarch's name in defamatory or insulting terms, and even nonverbal actions such as urinating or defecating on a picture of the royal person (such things happened!), constituted the crime of *lèse-majesté*. Until the early 18th century, publishers were required to obtain a government license in order to print their fare.

Newspapers were a constant source of tension between American colonists and British authorities. *Publick Occurrences Both Forreign and Domestick,* the first American newspaper, appeared in Boston in 1690 and was shut down almost immediately for having the temerity to criticize the government without a proper license. James Franklin, the brother of Benjamin Franklin, was imprisoned for a time and had his paper, *The New-England Courant,* shut down in 1726 for publishing seditious libel. The most famous case, however, was the 1735 libel trial of *The New York Weekly Journal* publisher John Peter Zenger.

Zenger was arrested and brought up on the charge of seditious libel for printing editorials that criticized the conduct of the governor-general of the Province of New York, William Cosby. (Yes, the royal governor of New York was named Bill Cosby). Zenger's lawyers argued that truth should be a defense to the charge of seditious libel; when the judge overruled them, they urged the jury to disregard the law and acquit their client. After deliberating for less than ten minutes, the jury returned a not-guilty verdict in one of the first examples of blatant jury nullification in American history. Although the case carried no precedential value and newspaper censorship continued unabated throughout the colonial period and beyond, its underlying premises—the right to free speech and the notion that the truth is a defense to libel—eventually won the day.

Even passage of the First Amendment did not end government attempts to limit speech rights in America. Perhaps the single greatest example is the Alien and Sedition Acts, signed into law by President John Adams in 1798. This series of measures made it a federal crime to publish "false, scandalous, and malicious writing or writings against the Government of the United States, or either House of [Congress], or the President, with intent to defame [them] . . . or to stir up sedition within the United States." The laws were passed as an emergency measure during the "Quasi War" between the United States and France following the French Revolution; fear of French agents infiltrating the country in order to agitate and provoke unrest was rampant. Newly elected President Thomas Jefferson allowed most of the Alien and Sedition acts to expire in 1800, but one section remained on the books and is technically still there today. Called the Alien Enemies Act, this measure was the basis for press censorship during World War I and Japanese internment during World War II.

The Supreme Court never ruled on the constitutionality of the Alien and Sedition Acts, and government censorship continued unabated throughout the 19th century. During the 1830s and 1840s, the U.S. House of Representatives operated under a series of "gag rule" resolutions that forbade members from discussing slavery or bringing up petitions that had anything to do with abolishing or restricting the practice. A number of states passed anti-literacy laws that prohibited black people from being taught how to read and write or being

allowed to speak publicly. Many Southern states also criminalized the publication and dissemination of abolitionist literature. Even passage of the Fourteenth Amendment after the Civil War did little to advance the idea that free speech is a constitutionally protected right for everyone throughout the United States. It would not be until the early 20th century and the outbreak of World War I that the Supreme Court finally stepped in.

"To suppress free speech is a double wrong. It violates the rights of the hearer as well as the speaker."
—Frederick Douglass

# ✦ 9 ✦

## CLEAR AND PRESENT DANGER
## (WITHOUT TOM CLANCY OR
## HARRISON FORD)

ONGRESS PASSED THE ESPIONAGE ACT OF 1917 AT
the urging of President Woodrow Wilson upon the United
States' entry into World War I. The Espionage Act made it a
federal crime to convey false reports, attempt to cause insubordination
or refusal of duty in the armed forces, or "willfully obstruct the recruit-
ing or enlistment service of the United States." This legislation was
amended the following year by the Sedition Act, which significantly
expanded the scope of the crime to include the use of "disloyal, pro-
fane, scurrilous, or abusive language" about the U.S. government, flag,

or armed forces, or to "willfully advocate, teach, defend, or suggest" anything that might favor the cause of an enemy nation in wartime.

The Espionage and Sedition Acts were far from toothless warnings to potential dissidents or ways to rally a divided public around the flag. More than 2,000 people would be convicted of violating these laws, and many served lengthy prison sentences. In 1919, the Supreme Court agreed to hear a handful of cases challenging the constitutionality of the acts, the most famous of which were *Schenck v. United States* and *Abrams v. United States*.

*Schenck* involved a challenge to the Espionage Act by two men who were convicted of illegally distributing pamphlets to new draftees that described conscription as being akin to slavery, urging draftees "not [to] submit to intimidation" and to "Assert Your Rights." A unanimous Supreme Court voted to uphold their convictions, finding that the free speech restrictions in the Espionage Act did not violate the First Amendment. Even if you had never read a Supreme Court decision before, you've almost certainly heard some of the highly quotable language used in the majority decision by Justice Oliver Wendell Holmes:

> *The most stringent protection of free speech would not protect a man in falsely shouting fire in a theatre and causing a panic. . . . [T]he question in every case is whether the words are used in such circumstances and are of such a nature as to create a clear and present danger that they will bring about the substantive evils that Congress has a right to prevent. It is a question of proximity and degree.*

Holmes's opinion continued with some cryptic remarks suggesting that the Court might have taken a different approach if the same restrictions had applied in peacetime. For example, "When a nation is at war many things that might be said in time of peace are such a hindrance to its effort that their utterance will not be endured so long as men fight, and no Court could regard them as protected by any constitutional right."

The Supreme Court unanimously affirmed two more convictions under the Espionage Act that same year, using the reasoning outlined in *Schenck*. Yet when it took up *Abrams v. United States*, its final Espionage Act case of the term, something strange happened. Justice Holmes appeared to have second thoughts about the broad scope of speech criminalization he had allowed in *Schenck*.

The facts in *Abrams* were slightly different than in the other cases. The Espionage and Sedition Acts specifically criminalized acts of resistance related to the war effort against the German Empire, but the defendants in *Abrams* were convicted of distributing pamphlets protesting U.S. military intervention against the Bolsheviks during the Russian Revolution. A seven-justice majority summarily upheld the convictions, but Justices Holmes and Louis Brandeis thought the Court had finally gone too far.

Holmes broke from his prior reasoning to deliver one of the most passionate defenses of the First Amendment in Supreme Court history. While he didn't argue for a reversal of *Schenck,* which he called "rightly decided," everything in his dissent slams the actions of the government. It was as if Justice Holmes had reluctantly allowed the government to criminalize certain speech as a wartime measure (Lincoln had done the same, and Holmes might have been sympathetic as a Civil War veteran) but was disappointed when it abused that power. Now Holmes defined clear and present danger more precisely as "danger of immediate evil or an intent to bring it about." Thus, he wrote, Congress cannot forbid any "silly leaflet by an unknown man" that expresses opinions it happens to disagree with. The purpose of the First Amendment is to allow for the free exchange of ideas, since:

> *the best test of truth [is] the power of the thought to get itself accepted in the competition of the market. . . . That at any rate is the theory of our Constitution. It is an experiment, as all life is an experiment.*

Holmes explicitly rejected the government's argument that the "First Amendment left the common law as to seditious libel in force." Instead, he insisted, we must be "eternally vigilant against attempts to

check the expression of opinions that we loathe," unless "an immediate check is required to save the country."

Something changed in Justice Holmes after his dissent in *Abrams*. He went from the mastermind of *Schenck* to one of the most ardent defenders of free speech rights. From that point on, Holmes would dissent from nearly every decision affirming a conviction under the Espionage and Sedition Acts. The shift came none too soon, as the United States entered its First Red Scare during the 1920s. Following the success of the Russian Revolution, which established the Soviet Union in 1922, the U.S. government began the mass deportation of aliens suspected of harboring communist sympathies. Nearly two-thirds of the states passed laws that criminalized advocating for communism as "criminal anarchy" or "criminal syndicalism."

The case of *Gitlow v. New York* (1925) concerned a challenge to one such state law. The defendant had published a document entitled "The Left Wing Manifesto" that advocated a communist overthrow of the U.S. government by mobilizing the "power of the proletariat in action." He was tried and convicted of violating New York's criminal anarchy statute, which made it a crime to "advocate, advise, or teach the duty, necessity or propriety of overthrowing or overturning organized government by force or violence."

The first issue for the Supreme Court was to determine whether the First Amendment should apply to the states. They held that yes, the Fourteenth Amendment incorporates the free speech protections of the First Amendment to the states since, they are "among the fundamental personal rights and 'liberties' protected by the due process clause of the Fourteenth Amendment from impairment by the States." With that out of the way, the justices moved on to the question of whether New York's criminal anarchy statute passed constitutional muster. Strangely enough, they did not apply the Clear and Present Danger Test from *Schenck*. Instead, the majority announced a new and extremely deferential standard that upheld all restrictions on speech

> *when the legislative body has determined . . . that utterances of a certain kind involve such danger of substantive evil that they may be punished.*

After all, wrote Justice Edward Sanford for the majority: "A single revolutionary spark may kindle a fire that, smoldering for a time, may burst into a sweeping and destructive conflagration. . . . It cannot be said that the State is acting arbitrarily or unreasonably when . . . it seeks to extinguish the spark."

Justices Holmes and Brandeis dissented against such a limited reading of the First Amendment. Asserting that "every idea is an incitement," Justice Holmes feared that the Court's decision would allow the government to criminalize *any* dangerous speech, no matter how remote the danger. Holmes reiterated his approach from *Abrams* that only speech designed to bring about imminent harm can be criminalized without violating the First Amendment.

The case of *Whitney v. California,* decided a few years later in 1927, dealt with many of the same issues as *Gitlow.* The defendant in *Whitney* had been convicted under California's criminal syndicalism statute for attempting to create the Communist Labor Party of America. A seven-justice majority again whittled the First Amendment down to almost nothing, holding that the authority of legislatures to punish "abuse" of freedom of speech such as "utterances inimical to public welfare, tending to incite crime, disturb the public peace, or endanger the foundations of organized government and threaten its overthrow by unlawful means," is "not open to question." In other words, if the legislature is acting to reduce crime, threats to the public order, or anything it views as contrary to the general welfare, it can criminalize speech. What *wouldn't* fall into such broad categories?

Justice Brandeis, in a concurring opinion joined by Justice Holmes, acknowledged that while "the rights of free speech and assembly are fundamental, they are not in their nature absolute." Getting down to particulars, he went on, "fear of serious injury cannot alone justify suppression of free speech and assembly. . . . Only an emergency can justify repression." Unlike the majority's deferential approach of limiting speech only that displayed "bad tendencies," Brandeis argued that freedom of speech is necessary for a self-governing citizenry:

> *[The] freedom to think as you will and to speak as you think are means indispensable to the discovery and spread of political truth; . . . public discussion is a political duty and this should be a fundamental principle of the American government. . . . [N]o danger flowing from speech can be deemed clear and present, unless the incidence of the evil apprehended is so imminent that it may befall before there is opportunity for full discussion.*

The attitude of the high court toward free speech began to shift in the 1930s. Perhaps due to the political climate brought on by the Great Depression or the persuasive dissents of Justices Holmes and Brandeis, a majority of the justices began to turn away from *Gitlow* and *Whitney* toward a more exacting standard for laws that restrict speech. In the two 1937 cases of *De Jonge v. Oregon* and *Herndon v. Lowery,* the Supreme Court overturned criminal syndicalism convictions on First Amendment grounds. The defendant in *De Jonge* was convicted for participating in a meeting of the Communist Party, but a unanimous Supreme Court ruled in his favor, finding that mere participation in political activities cannot be made a crime absent actual advocacy of violently overthrowing the government. The defendant in *Herndon* was a member of the Communist Party of Atlanta who had been convicted of attempting to "incite insurrection" for possessing pamphlets calling for "black self-determination." A 5–4 Supreme Court struck down the law on the grounds that it was both unconstitutionally vague and overly broad in scope (potentially punishable by death!).

Joseph McCarthy

No sooner had the Court started to expand freedom of speech protections than the pendulum swung back the other way. World War II was over, but the Cold War had begun—and along with it the Second Red Scare. The House of Representatives used its Un-American Activities Committee to investigate Communist infiltration into American life, and Senator Joseph McCarthy conducted similar hearings in the Senate. In 1950, with tensions running high, Congress passed the Subversive Activities Control Act (overriding President Harry Truman's veto), requiring all Communists to register with the U.S. Attorney General's

Office. Against this backdrop, a number of Communist Party leaders were arrested and tried for violation of the Smith Act, a federal equivalent to the New York criminal anarchy statute challenged in *Gitlow*.

Among those convicted of violating the Smith Act was Eugene Dennis, the secretary-general of the Communist Party of the United States. In the case of *Dennis v. United States* (1951), a divided Supreme Court decided by a 6–2 margin to uphold his conviction. No single opinion was able to command a majority of the justices. The four-justice plurality opinion, written by Chief Justice Fred Vinson, declared that *Gitlow* and *Whitney* were still binding precedents even though he acknowledged that recent decisions had been "inclined towards the Holmes-Brandeis rationale." Applying a slightly modified Clear and Present Danger Test, the plurality determined that the grave threat posed to American society by international Communism justified the restrictions on speech: "[I]f the ingredients of the reaction are present, we cannot bind the Government to wait until the catalyst is added."

Justice Robert Jackson, writing in concurrence, argued for an even more deferential standard. The Clear and Present Danger Test might be good for most free speech cases, he maintained, but it arose before the "subtlety and efficacy of modernized revolutionary techniques used by totalitarian parties." With evident alarm, Jackson argued that the government must be given every tool available to win the fight against Communism "during its period of incubation." To do otherwise would restrict the government from acting "only after imminent action is manifest, when it would, of course, be too late."

Justices William Douglas and Hugo Black each filed separate dissents. They would do so repeatedly in free speech cases, as they were the only two First Amendment absolutists ever to sit on the Supreme Court. In their view, the statement "Congress shall make no law . . . abridging the freedom of speech" meant quite literally that any restriction on speech violates the Constitution. Justice Douglas was dismissive of the Communist threat, calling party members "miserable merchants of unwanted ideas" and comparing the books of Marx, Engels, and Lenin to Hitler's *Mein Kampf.* If they are widely read rather than restricted, he wrote, "the ugliness of Communism is revealed, its deceit and cunning are exposed, the nature of its activities becomes apparent, and the chances of its success less likely."

Justice Black's dissent was short and direct. He would have overturned not only the convictions, but the entire Smith Act, for violating the First Amendment. In spite of his obvious disappointment over the outcome of the case, he ended his dissent on an optimistic note: "There is hope, however, that in calmer times, when present pressures, passions and fears subside, this or some later Court will restore the First

Amendment liberties to the high preferred place where they belong in a free society."

He wouldn't have to wait long. Although *Dennis* opened the floodgates to prosecutions of more than 130 members of the Communist Party under the Smith Act, the Supreme Court took a different direction only six years later in *Yates v. United States* (1957). A lot had happened in the meantime. Senator McCarthy's anti-Communist crusade ended with his official censure in 1954 and his death in 1957. Public opinion also shifted away from the need for censorship as the Red Scare began to fade.

In *Yates,* the Supreme Court overturned fourteen Smith Act convictions of Communists. Although the justices did not invalidate the Smith Act for violating the First Amendment, they severely neutered it by holding that it can criminalize only "advocacy of action," not "advocacy of abstract doctrine." Under new Chief Justice Earl Warren, the Court was clearly signaling a different approach on First Amendment issues. And so, throughout the 1960s, it chipped away at the Smith Act, the Subversive Activities Control Act, and other federal attempts to ban the Communist Party and criminalize the dissemination of Communist literature without explicitly overruling their prior cases. That came to an end in the 1969 case of *Brandenburg v. Ohio.*

The challenger in *Brandenburg* was the leader of the Ohio chapter of the Ku Klux Klan, who had been arrested, charged, and convicted of violating Ohio's criminal syndicalism statute for threatening at a rally to take "revengeance [sic]" against the president, Congress, and Supreme Court if they continued "to suppress the white, Caucasian race."

The language was especially inflammatory in the context of the time, following the assassinations of President John F. Kennedy in 1963, Malcolm X in 1965, and Dr. Martin Luther King and Robert Kennedy in 1968.

Until then, the Supreme Court had usually folded when the threat level was running high, deferring to legislative judgments about what kinds of speech are dangerous enough to criminalize. *Whitney* had turned the First Amendment into little more than a nice idea by allowing the government to criminalize speech whenever the legislature determined that it ran contrary to the public welfare. In *Brandenburg*, however, the justices made a unanimous course correction, both overturning the conviction and striking down Ohio's criminal syndicalism statute (and by extension all similar statutes in other states) for violating the First Amendment. They also discarded *Whitney* without ambiguity, ruling definitively that "mere advocacy" or "abstract teaching," no matter how potentially dangerous the message or insidious the content, can never constitute a crime. The only time that the government can criminalize speech, they now held, is when it is "directed to inciting or producing imminent lawless action and is likely to incite or produce such action."

This Brandenburg Test, while sounding similar to the Clear and Present Danger Test, is actually much closer to strict scrutiny in practice and remains in use to the present day. The Supreme Court would no longer defer to the judgement of legislatures regarding the "bad tendencies" of certain types of speech. For speech to be criminal, the government would have to prove that the speaker intended to incite imminent lawless action and that such action was likely to occur. This severely restricts the types of speech that can be banned and is perhaps what Justice Holmes had in mind with his famous example of shouting fire in a crowded theater. Under *Brandenburg*, urging a rioting mob to murder police officers is criminal, but advocating their murder in an inflammatory blog post is constitutionally protected speech.

# ✦ 10 ✦

## THERE'S A TIME, PLACE, AND MANNER FOR EVERYTHING: FREE SPEECH IN PUBLIC PLACES AND ON GOVERNMENT PROPERTY

WE NOW KNOW THAT THE FIRST AMENDMENT SETS a high bar for the government to criminalize speech. But does it also require the government to guarantee an open forum for people to exercise their free speech rights? Can the government regulate what kinds of speech happen in public places like parks, street corners, city halls, or courthouses because it "owns" the property? These questions raise a host of broader issues, such as how to balance free speech rights against other public interests, like safety, good order, and peace and quiet. And even further, does the Constitution prohibit the government from doing things that interfere only with individual rights (the "negative rights" interpretation), or does it require the government to enable individuals to exercise their rights (the "positive rights" interpretation)?

The first time the Supreme Court ruled on a public forum issue was in the 1895 case of *Davis v. Massachusetts*. The city of Boston required all persons wishing to speak in public to obtain a permit from the mayor. Much like the Jehovah's Witnesses in *Cantwell*, a pastor decided to disregard the law and preached openly on the Boston Common. He was summarily arrested and convicted of violating the city ordinance. Our old friend Oliver Wendell Holmes—not yet on the Supreme Court but serving on the highest court in Massachusetts—upheld the conviction, likening the city's ownership of Boston Common to that of a private proprietor. Davis appealed this to the Supreme Court, which unanimously affirmed Holmes's decision. Yes, the government had the absolute right to regulate speech on public property, just as a private owner did. That remained the rule for more than forty years, until *Hague v. CIO* (1939).

At issue in *Hague* was a Jersey City ordinance that prevented organized labor advocates from speaking or pamphleteering in public spaces. The Committee for Industrial Organization (CIO, a federation of unions) sued to block the ordinance, and the case came before the U.S. Supreme Court. Justice Owen Roberts, writing the opinion of the Court, overruled *Davis* and announced a new rule: Streets, parks, and other such places belong to a "public forum" that the government has held "from ancient times . . . in trust for the use of the public . . . for purposes of assembly, communicating thoughts between citizens, and discussing public questions." The government may regulate speech in these public areas "in the interest of all," but it may not abridge or deny speech "in the guise of regulation." The Supreme Court thus agreed with Justice Holmes that the government owns the property in question, but likened the public to having a "kind of First-Amendment easement" to use the property for purposes of speech.

Quick definition: in property law, an **easement** is a right-of-way over another person's land. For instance, if your driveway cuts through your neighbor's property, that's an easement.

And so, after *Hague*, we were left with an all-too-familiar dilemma. The Supreme Court announced a new rule that sounded nice but was left pretty vague: Public property should be open and available for speech, but the government is free to regulate it in the public interest as long as the excuse is not a sham. How are we supposed to determine this, exactly? On its face, this rule seems to give government officials a lot of discretion regarding what kinds of speech to allow on public property.

The Court tried to add a little clarity two years later in the case of *Cox v. New Hampshire* (1941). Here, several Jehovah's Witnesses were convicted of violating a state law by marching down a public street without having first obtained a permit. Unlike in prior cases, the justices now

**TRADITIONAL PUBLIC FORA**

**DESIGNATED (or limited) PUBLIC FORA**

**NON PUBLIC FORA**

came down on the side of the state, holding that regulation of traffic is a "traditional exercise" of government power and that "the question in a particular case is whether [the government's action] is exerted so as not to deny or unwarrantedly abridge the right of assembly and [speech]." In its ruling, the Court set forth criteria to help determine whether the government's regulation of speech is permissible. First, there must be objective standards in place employing "uniformity of method of treatment" that does not rely on "arbitrary power or an unfettered discretion" on the part of officials. Second, the restrictions must not concern the content of the speech, but only the time, place, and manner in which it takes place. Because the New Hampshire statute was content-neutral and was applied uniformly and non-arbitrarily in order to regulate the time, place, and manner of speech, it did not violate the First Amendment.

While *Cox v. New Hampshire* did not resolve all potential issues, it did set the foundation of what would become known as "time, place, and manner" or TPM doctrine. This requires courts to engage in a balancing test, weighing the needs of the public to use the space for free and open speech against the interests of the government in maintaining order. The key here is that any restrictions on speech can regulate only the time, place, and manner in which the speech takes place. It must not discriminate on the basis of what the speakers say, and the standards for granting licenses must be objective and non-arbitrary.

An example of a law regulating speech that appeared to be neutral but was applied in an unconstitutional way was seen in the 1965 case of *Cox v. Louisiana* (no relation to *Cox v. New Hampshire*, just a strange coincidence). In this case, a number of black protestors who were picketing in front of a segregated restaurant were arrested, charged, and convicted for breach of peace. Even though the relevant statute was facially neutral and placed a seemingly absolute restriction on impeding the "free, convenient and normal use of any public sidewalk, street, [or] other passageway," it also allowed cities to issue permits for parades and street demonstrations. There was nothing inherently wrong with the statute, but it contained no standards for determining when a permit should be issued, leaving it up to the "uncontrolled discretion" of local officials. This allowed the official to "act as a censor" for speech, and—guess what?—no permit had ever been issued to civil rights demonstrators. The Supreme Court overturned the convictions of the picketers.

Streets, sidewalks, and parks are obvious examples of government property that constitute "public fora" for purposes of free speech. But what about other types of public property, such as schools, libraries, courthouses, jails, and government offices? Is any public property necessarily a public forum that must be made open and available for speech? The 1972 case of *Grayned v. Rockford* answered this question. Richard Grayned was a civil rights protestor who was arrested, tried, and convicted for violating an Illinois town's anti-picketing ordinance, which forbade any demonstrations within 150 feet of a school currently in session. Justice Thurgood Marshall, writing on behalf of

a near-unanimous Court (one justice dissented in part), upheld the constitutionality of both the conviction and the statute. The justices concluded that it was "the nature of the place [and] the pattern of its normal activities" that should determine whether the time, place, and manner restrictions are reasonable. "The crucial question," Marshall wrote, is "whether the manner of expression is basically incompatible with the normal activity of a particular place at a particular time." Even though the sidewalks in front of the school are public property, the government need not "tolerate boisterous demonstrators who drown out classroom conversation, making studying impossible, block entrances, or incite children to leave the schoolhouse." To permit otherwise would interfere with student learning, the very reason for the school's existence.

*Grayned*, along with separate cases upholding restrictions on speech in jails, military bases, libraries, and mailboxes, stand for the proposition that the First Amendment does not guarantee speakers access to any public property just because it is owned by the government. The Supreme Court was clearly moving in the direction of a classification scheme for speech on public property, and it arrived there in the 1983 case of *Perry Education Association v. Perry Local Educators' Association*.

*Perry* concerned a clause in a collective bargaining agreement between the teachers' union and an Indiana town that restricted a rival teachers' group from using the school's internal mail system for advocacy. In a 5–4 decision, Justice Byron White delivered the majority opinion upholding the mailing restrictions. Even though the clause was not content-neutral, the Court found that it passed constitutional muster. Why? Because both "the existence of a right of access to public property" and the standard used to evaluate restrictions on that access "differ depending on the character of the property at issue."

The Supreme Court divided all public property into three broad categories. The first category, requiring the highest level of First Amendment scrutiny, is called **traditional public fora**. These are the kinds of places, such as street corners, parks, and town squares, that "by long tradition or government fiat" have been open to public assembly. The Supreme Court had afforded these "quintessential public forums" a high degree of protection since way back in *Hague*, but now the majority made the extent of that protection clear: The government cannot prohibit speech in these areas, must satisfy strict scrutiny if it wants to enforce a content-based restriction, and must justify even content-neutral TPM restrictions by showing that they serve a "significant" government interest and leave open "ample alternative channels of communication." In other words, the restrictions must be "narrowly tailored."

The second category is called **"designated" or limited public fora**. These are public properties that do not qualify as traditional public fora but that the government has opened up to expressive activity. A good example is a community center open to the public. The government is not required to create these spaces or even to keep them open, but as long as they do, they must treat them like a traditional public forum.

The third category, **nonpublic fora**, consists of any other type public property that does not fall into one of the first two categories. Here the government can restrict any speech as long as the restriction is reasonable and not "an effort to suppress expression merely because public officials oppose the speaker's view."

After *Perry*, the big question in most TPM cases is what category the public property falls into. Regulating speech in a traditional public forum is very difficult to sustain, whereas anything reasonable and nondiscriminatory will pass muster in a nonpublic forum. That's not to say that sorting public property into three tidy boxes is always easy or obvious. The court has struggled with how to classify government-owned office buildings, entrances to post offices, public transportation hubs, and airport terminals. Even when a majority of the justices agrees on how to classify a public forum, there is still a lot of ambiguity in determining what kinds of government interests qualify as "compelling" or "significant" and just how much "narrow tailoring" is enough. A good example of how the Supreme Court resolved this conundrum is the 1989 case of *Ward v. Rock Against Racism*.

New York City had passed an ordinance that required any musical acts performing in Central Park to use city-provided acoustic equipment and sound technicians in order to keep the volume level in check. The musical group Rock Against Racism, which had put on yearly concerts in Central Park, challenged the ordinance on the grounds that it interfered with its free speech right to artistic expression. The case reached the U.S. Supreme Court, where all nine justices agreed that the area was definitely a traditional public forum, that New York's interest in limiting excessive noise in Central Park was compelling, and that the ordinance was content-neutral. The only question left to resolve was whether the regulation was narrowly tailored enough.

The Second Circuit had interpreted the narrow-tailoring requirement to mean that the ordinance must be the least speech-restrictive way of accomplishing the government's goal, and it struck down the New York ordinance for being overly broad. A seven-justice majority of the Supreme Court rejected this view. Justice Kennedy, writing for the majority, specified that "narrow tailoring is satisfied so long as the regulation . . . promotes a substantial government interest that would be achieved less effectively absent the regulation . . . [and] is not substantially broader than necessary to achieve the government's interest." Based on this reasoning, the Court will usually approve content-neutral TPM restrictions in a traditional public forum when the government makes at least some attempt to limit its scope.

But what happens when the government acts to restrict free speech on public property in order to protect the exercise of other constitutional rights, such as the right to obtain an abortion? The U.S. Supreme Court has attempted to resolve this question on three separate occasions: in *Madsen v. Women's Health Center, Inc.* (1994), *Hill v. Colorado* (2000), and *McCullen v. Coakley* (2014).

The *Madsen* case arose from a Florida abortion clinic's attempt to stop a group of protestors from picketing on a public street in front of its entrance. The trial court issued an injunction prohibiting the protestors from approaching within thirty-six feet of the entrance, along with other provisions that barred them from shouting at, displaying graphic images to, or physically approaching people seeking services at the clinic. The Supreme Court, in a horribly disjointed decision full of partial dissents and concurrences, upheld the part of the injunction related to the thirty-six-foot barrier and some noise prohibitions as valid TPM restrictions, while striking down the rest. Most importantly for our purposes is that a majority of the Court recognized the significant state interest in "protecting a woman's freedom to seek lawful medical or counseling services in connection with her pregnancy."

*Hill* went a step further in addressing a Colorado statute that prohibited anyone within 100 feet of any healthcare facility from approaching within eight feet of another person without that person's consent, "for the purpose of passing a leaflet or handbill to, displaying a sign to, or engaging in oral protest, education, or counselling." Since the statute restricted speech in a public forum, the outcome of the case would rest on whether a majority of the justices found the restriction to be content-based (requiring strict scrutiny) or content-neutral. Justice John Paul Stevens delivered the seven-justice majority opinion, upholding the statute as a content-neutral TPM restriction. According to the majority, the law did not regulate speech per se, but only "the places where some speech may occur." The Court also recognized a significant state interest in protecting patients seeking healthcare services from unwanted harassment. Finally, it held that the restriction was narrowly tailored, satisfying the *Ward* test by not being substantially broader than needed and leaving alternate channels of communication open to the protestors. Justices Scalia and Thomas issued a vigorous dissent, slamming the idea that the government has a significant interest in protecting people from unwanted communication (which would make "the First Amendment a dead letter") and criticizing the majority's narrow tailoring analysis: "Narrow tailoring must refer not to the standards of Versace, but to those of Omar the tentmaker."

The most recent case is *McCullen v. Coakley* (2014). In an effort to cut down on confrontations between protestors and women seeking abortions, Massachusetts had passed a law in 2007 that established thirty-five-foot buffer zones in front of the entrance to all reproductive healthcare facilities. An antiabortion group sued, claiming that the buffer zones blocked their efforts to engage in "sidewalk counseling" with women entering the clinics. Although the Supreme Court found the buffer zones to be content-neutral TPM restrictions that furthered a significant state interest, all nine justices voted to strike down the law because they concluded that, unlike in *Hill*, the regulation was not narrowly tailored. The key difference between the two

cases is that the law in *Hill* only prohibited people from approaching
within eight feet without consent,
whereas the thirty-five-foot buffer
zone effectively blocked all efforts
by antiabortion advocates to engage in
one-on-one communication with patients
entering the clinic. The Court also firmed up

the definition of narrow tailoring, requiring the state to demonstrate
that "alternative measures that burden substantially less speech would
fail to achieve the government's interests, not simply that the chosen
route is easier."

This is where the law has stood since 2014. Although there will
always be some ambiguity, TPM restrictions constitute one of the most
settled and predicable areas of First Amendment case law. Just keep these
basic principles in mind: Content-neutral TPM restrictions in a traditional or designated public forum require the restriction to be narrowly
tailored to serve a significant government interest—meaning that less
speech-restrictive alternatives would not achieve the same goal—and to
leave open other alternative channels of communication (content-based
restrictions must always pass strict scrutiny), while the government may
prohibit any expression in a nonpublic forum as long as the restriction
is reasonable and not designed merely to oppose a specific viewpoint.

# ✦ 11 ✦

## FREE SPEECH FOR THE DUMB: "FIGHTING WORDS," PROVOCATION, HOSTILE AUDIENCES, AND HATE SPEECH

Wait! These aren't candles!

**A**CLOSE COUSIN TO THE INCITEMENT CASES DIS-
cussed back in Chapter 9 are those dealing with "fighting
words," provocation, hostile audiences, and hate speech. The
question here is whether the government can criminalize speech that
is likely to outrage an audience and lead to a violent response. Does
the government's interest in maintaining public order allow it to prohibit a person from saying offensive things that are likely to result in
him being punched, or does the First Amendment protect the right

to provoke others? We will also talk here about hate speech and the extent to which the First Amendment protects the right of racists, bigots, and misogynists to express their opinions.

The Supreme Court addressed the question of fighting words in the landmark 1942 case of *Chaplinsky v. New Hampshire*. Walter Chaplinsky, a Jehovah's Witness (yet again!), caused a disturbance when he began preaching in public that organized religion was a "racket." The police led him away from the crowd, and Chaplinksy got into an argument with the city marshall, saying that he had the right to be there and that the police should have arrested the people in the crowd for causing the disturbance. When the marshall disagreed, Chaplinsky called him a "God damned racketeer" and "a damned Fascist," and claimed that "the whole government of Rochester are Fascists or agents of Fascists." Chaplinsky was duly arrested, charged, and convicted of violating New Hampshire's offensive conduct statute, which made it a crime for anyone to address "any offensive, derisive or annoying word to any other person who is lawfully in any street or public place, [or] call him by an offensive or derisive name."

A unanimous Supreme Court voted to affirm the conviction. In a brief opinion, Justice Frank Murphy penned one of the most important paragraphs in the history of First Amendment case law:

> [I]t is well understood that the right of free speech is not absolute at all times and under all circumstances. There are certain well-defined and narrowly limited classes of speech, the prevention and punishment of which has never been thought to raise any Constitutional problem. These include the lewd and obscene, the profane, the libelous, and the insulting or "fighting" words—those which by their very utterance inflict injury or tend to incite an immediate breach of the peace. It has been well observed that such utterances are no essential part of any exposition of ideas, and are of such slight social value as a step to truth that any benefit that may be derived from them is clearly outweighed by the social interest in order and morality. Resort to epithets or personal abuse is not in any proper sense communication of information or opinion safeguarded by the Constitution, and its punishment as a criminal act would raise no question under that instrument.

More simply put, not all speech qualifies for constitutional protection. Things like obscenity, libel, and fighting words fall wholly outside the First Amendment, allowing the government to regulate them with impunity, like traffic patterns or water rights. Fighting words, according to Justice Murphy, are those that "men of common intelligence would understand [to be] words likely to cause an average addressee to fight." Construed in this way, the New Hampshire statute was designed to criminalize language that might provoke others to commit violent acts and lead to public disturbance. Even though what Chaplinsky said might not qualify as "classical fighting words" (the Court left it open to the reader to imagine what they might be), it still passed the test—remember, he was flinging around fascist accusations soon after the U.S. entry into World War II.

Where did the idea come from that certain kinds of speech don't qualify as "speech"? The first reason the Court gave for this non-obvious interpretation of the First Amendment was a blanket assertion: It is "well understood," they said, that certain types of speech can be regulated or prohibited and that this "has never been thought to raise any Constitutional problem." The second, more substantive reason was that on balance there are certain types of speech whose social and informational value is so slight that the right of people to indulge in them is "clearly outweighed by the social interest in order and morality."

It is WELL UNDERSTOOD that certain words are fighting words.

"Well understood" by whom?

Are you starting something?

The big idea here is that the First Amendment protects speech on a sliding scale of social utility. Fighting words, libel, obscenity, and the like have little in the way of verbal nutritional content yet come with a high tendency to degrade social order and morality. Thus, they should not be afforded the same degree of protection as more highbrow forms, such as political speech. You might think this is a strange interpretation, but the Supreme Court has never overruled *Chaplinsky*, and we'll see it come up time and again in the chapters ahead.

One problem with the fighting words exception is that it would seem to allow offended people to exercise a "heckler's veto" by shutting down another person's free speech rights. No case demonstrates this better than *Feiner v. New York* (1951). The facts are particularly important here. In 1949, Feiner, a white college student, decided to stand on a wooden box with a loudspeaker on the street corner of a predominantly black neighborhood in Syracuse, NY. Once there, he announced that President Truman and the mayor of Syracuse were both "bums," that the American Legion was little more than "a Nazi Gestapo," and that "Negroes don't have equal rights; they should rise up in arms and fight for them." A mixed-race crowd of about eighty people had gathered around Feiner and started to become agitated. When police arrived on

the scene, one of the onlookers told the arresting officer, "If you don't get that son of a bitch off, I will go over and get him off there myself." The police told Feiner that he was causing a disturbance and asked him three times to get down and stop speaking. When he refused, he was arrested for violating New York's disorderly conduct statute, of which he was later tried and convicted.

The U.S. Supreme Court voted 6-3 to uphold Feiner's conviction. Justice Fred Vinson, writing for the majority, argued that Feiner was not arrested for the content of his speech but because of "the reaction which it actually engendered." The principle is similar to the fighting words exemption to the First Amendment and is often called the "hostile audiences rule." Although the majority expressed concern that "the ordinary murmurings and objections of a hostile audience cannot be allowed to silence a speaker" and were "mindful of the possible danger of giving overzealous police officials complete discretion to break up otherwise lawful public meetings," they still concluded that "the imminence of greater disorder coupled with [Feiner's] deliberate defiance of the police officers convince us that we should not reverse [the conviction]."

Justice Black argued in dissent that the majority's analysis was misguided. Rather than hold Feiner accountable, the Court should have put the blame on the police for failing "to protect [his] constitutional right to talk." In Justice Black's view, the police had no right to ask Feiner to stop speaking, and his refusal to comply with their illegitimate order did not constitute "deliberate defiance." Black explained further: "On the contrary, I think that the policeman's action was a 'deliberate defiance' of ordinary official duty as well as of the constitutional right of free speech."

The Supreme Court continued its hostile-audiences approach the following year in the case of *Beauharnais v. Illinois* (1952). Beauharnais, a white supremacist, published a pamphlet that called on white people to unite against "the further encroachment, harassment and invasion of white people, their property, neighborhoods and persons by the Negro" so as to "prevent the white race from becoming mongrelized."

Beauharnais was arrested, tried, and convicted of violating Illinois' group libel statute, which made it a crime to publish or exhibit material that "portrays depravity, criminality, unchastity, or lack of virtue of a class of citizens, of any race, color, creed, or religion . . . or which is productive of breach of the peace or riots."

A split 5–4 Supreme Court voted again to uphold the restriction on speech. The majority opinion, written by Justice Felix Frankfurter, cited *Chaplinky* and *Feiner* as authority for the proposition that certain types of speech are excluded from the protections of the First Amendment, "group libel" being one such exclusion. The majority contended that Illinois had experienced a history of "exacerbated tension between races, often flaring into violence and destruction," requiring government intervention in order to maintain "free, ordered life in a metropolitan, polyglot community." Justice Black dissented yet again, arguing that the First Amendment "'absolutely' forbids [group libel] laws without any 'ifs' or 'buts' or 'whereases.'"

The big shift happened in the 1971 case of *Cohen v. California*. As you may have noticed by now, Supreme Court decisions are often influenced as much by current events and politics as they are by law and precedent. The country had undergone tectonic cultural shifts during the 1960s, and the Supreme Court went right along with it. Rapid changes in public attitudes toward race relations, sexual morality, and political protest had made the United States of 1970 barely recognizable by 1950s standards. Turmoil over the Vietnam War had also exposed deep fissures in a country that appeared to be coming apart at the seams.

In the spring of 1968, during the bloodiest year in Vietnam, nineteen-year-old Paul Cohen entered a Los Angeles courthouse wearing a jacket with the words "Fuck the Draft" emblazoned across the back. Cohen was arrested and charged with violating California's public disturbance statute for engaging in "offensive conduct . . . which has a tendency to provoke others to acts of violence or to in turn disturb the peace." California convicted him on the grounds that "it was certainly reasonably foreseeable that such conduct might cause others to rise up to commit a violent act against [him] or attempt to forcibly remove his jacket."

In another 5–4 decision, a majority of the Supreme Court reversed course from previous rulings. Although part of what Cohen did was demonstrative, the majority decided that his decision to wear the jacket was indeed a form of constitutionally protected speech rather than "conduct" the state could regulate. His speech was not intended to "incite disobedience to or disruption of the draft," the justices held, but only to express his belief on its "inutility or immorality." They also ruled out the possibility that the California statute was a content-neutral TPM restriction because it was applicable "throughout the entire State," with no specific language limiting it to certain places like courthouses.

Then they got to the classes of unprotected speech mentioned in *Chaplinsky*. Even though Cohen's jacket displayed profanity, the majority concluded that the words did not qualify as obscenity, since "such expression must be, in some significant way, erotic" (more about obscenity in Chapter 13). They also ruled out the fighting words exception, since the message was "clearly not 'directed to the person of the hearer,'" and "no individual actually or likely to be present could reasonably have regarded the words . . . as a direct personal insult." Nor did the message qualify for the hostile audience exception, since there was "no showing that anyone who saw Cohen was in fact violently aroused or that [he] intended such a result." Finally, the Court dismissed the state's claim that it was protecting unwilling viewers, since that "would effectively empower a majority to silence dissidents simply as a matter of personal predilection" by exercising a heckler's veto. The people in the courthouse were not in any sense a captive audience, and those offended by Cohen's message could avoid it "simply by averting their eyes."

Since none of the exceptions were deemed applicable to this case, the Court could only analyze Cohen's conviction as a content-based restriction on speech. The majority found unconvincing California's argument that the word "fuck" should be excluded from First Amendment protections: "How is one to distinguish this from any other offensive word?" they asked. Since "one man's vulgarity is another's lyric," the First Amendment "leaves matters of taste and style largely to the individual." And so, the majority concluded, because the government cannot regulate mere "verbal tumult, discord, and even offensive utterance," Cohen's conviction should be overturned. The dissenters argued that Cohen's action of wearing the jacket inside a courthouse was conduct rather than speech and that, even if it was speech, it would fall "well within the sphere of *Chaplinsky*."

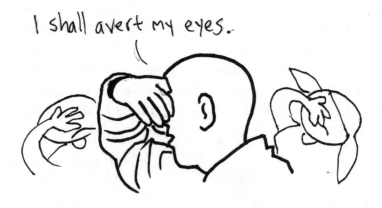

Where does hate speech fit in with all this? One could make the argument that *Chaplinsky* and *Feiner* allow the government to regulate hate speech under the fighting words or hostile audience exceptions to the First Amendment. Hate speech also seems similar to the Illinois group libel statute the Supreme Court let stand in *Beauharnais*. Maybe the Supreme Court should even carve out hate speech as a new category of unprotected speech under *Chaplinsky*, since "such utterances are no essential part of any exposition of ideas and are of such slight social value as a step to truth that any benefit that may be derived from them is clearly outweighed by the social interest in order and morality." That, however, would buck the Court's overall trend of recent decades in expanding the realm of protected free speech rights. All of these arguments came to a head in a series of cases known as the Skokie Affair.

Frank Collin, the leader of a Nazi group called the National Socialist Party of America (NSAP), began organizing antiblack demonstrations in Chicago's Marquette Park during the mid-1970s. Municipal authorities responded by passing ordinances that required demonstrators to obtain large liability and property damage insurance policies before being issued a permit. As the fight against the Chicago ordinances dragged on, Collin came up with an alternate scheme that would draw public attention to his efforts and possibly get his case in front of the Supreme Court. He announced that the NSAP would march through the streets of nearby Skokie, Illinois, a community with a large Jewish population, many of whom were Holocaust survivors. The village sued the NSAP to stop the group from marching, and the Illinois trial court issued an injunction prohibiting them from "parading in the [party] uniform . . . displaying the swastika . . . and distributing pamphlets . . . which incite or promote hatred against any person of any faith or ancestry, race or religion." The Illinois appellate and supreme courts both refused to stay the injunction or to order an expedited appeal. This meant that the injunction would stand for perhaps the next several years as the case made its way through the courts. The NSAP appealed that decision to the Supreme Court.

In the case of *National Socialist Party of America v. Village of Skokie* (1977), a six-justice majority voted to overturn the decision of the Illinois Supreme Court and stayed the injunction. While the Supreme Court did not answer the question of whether Skokie could constitutionally ban the NSAP from marching, it did decide that Illinois needed to conduct an "immediate appellate review" or else stay the injunction, since such a severe restriction of First Amendment rights must come with "strict procedural safeguards." Upon hearing the case again, the Illinois Supreme Court decided that "the display of the swastika cannot be enjoined" under either the fighting words or hostile audience exceptions to the First Amendment since anyone can "avoid the offensive symbol . . . without unreasonable inconvenience."

As soon as the Illinois Supreme Court lifted the injunction, the Village of Skokie enacted a series of ordinances to stop the march. The NSAP, ironically represented by a Jewish ACLU attorney, sued to have the Skokie ordinances overturned. The U.S. District Court struck down all of the ordinances for violating the First Amendment, and the U.S. Circuit Court affirmed that decision, even questioning whether "*Beauharnais* would pass constitutional muster today." The Supreme Court refused to stay the decision while deciding whether to review the case. The legal path was now clear for Frank Collin to lead his group of brown shirt-wearing, swastika flag-waving, goose-stepping Nazis through the streets of Skokie.

Except that he didn't do it. Three days before the march was set to take place, Collin canceled the entire affair. Skokie was never the target—Chicago was. He had selected Skokie, with its large Jewish population, as "pure agitation" to get his case in front of the courts. Now, with favorable rulings from both the U.S. and Illinois Supreme Courts, Collin was able to overturn Chicago's ordinances and demonstrate in the park. His small group of about twenty-five Nazis held their demonstration in July 1978 without incident.

The final postscript came when the U.S. Supreme Court declined to review the case any further. Justices Harry Blackmun and Byron White dissented, noting that the case would allow the Court to determine whether "there is no limit whatsoever to the exercise of free speech." Because the Skokie march was intentionally designed to be "taunting and overwhelmingly uncomfortable to the citizens of that place . . . [it] just might fall into the same category as one's 'right' to cry 'fire' in a crowded theatre." They also raised the question of whether the act of wearing Nazi uniforms and displaying the swastika was actually speech rather than conduct—something we'll talk about more in the next chapter.

The unsatisfying ending to the Skokie Affair mirrors the unsettled state of hate speech law in the United States. If anything, the Supreme Court and lower federal courts have erred on the side of protecting hate speech unless it falls into already-existing fighting words or hostile audiences exceptions. There is always a possibility that the Supreme Court might one day carve out a special First Amendment exception for hate speech, but such a prospect appears unlikely for the time being.

# ✦ 12 ✦

## BURNING FLAGS,
## DRAFT CARDS, AND CROSSES:
## SYMBOLIC SPEECH AND EXPRESSION

THE SUPREME COURT HAS STATED ON NUMEROUS occasions that the First Amendment protects only speech, not conduct. But what does that mean for nonverbal forms of communication that seek to express ideas through actions rather than words? What is the status of this "symbolic speech" under the First Amendment?

The Court has long recognized that symbolic speech deserves at least some protection. As far back as 1931, in the case of *Stromberg v. California*, the Court forbade the State of California from criminalizing the display of Communist red flags. In *Brown v. Louisiana* (1966), the justices ruled that a sit-in at a public library constitutes speech, since

First Amendment rights "are not confined to verbal expression" and "embrace appropriate types of action" as well. However, the Supreme Court did not establish a comprehensive framework to analyze symbolic speech until two years later in the case of *United States v. O'Brien* (1968).

By 1965, U.S. involvement in Vietnam was ramping up and the Selective Service had begun conscripting young men into the army. Opposition to both the war and the draft led some to burn their draft cards in protest. In response, Congress passed a law that made it a federal crime to "forge, alter, knowingly destroy, knowingly mutilate, or in any manner change" a draft card. On the morning of March 31, 1966, David Paul O'Brien burned his draft card on the steps of a Boston courthouse in front of a sizeable crowd. He was arrested, tried, and convicted for violating the statute.

The Supreme Court had two issues to consider here: First, is burning a draft card "speech" for purposes of the First Amendment? And if so, could the law banning it pass constitutional muster? Chief Justice Earl Warren delivered the 8-1 majority opinion. Although the Court had recognized that certain nonverbal actions qualify as "speech" since *Stromberg,* Warren emphasized that it could not grant the designation to "an apparently limitless variety of conduct." And so he formulated a test for determining the constitutionality of restrictions on symbolic speech. First, he wrote,

*when "speech" and "non-speech" elements are combined in the same course of conduct, a sufficiently important governmental interest in regulating the non-speech element can justify incidental limitations on First Amendment freedoms.*

This means that while symbolic speech is protected, the government has the right to regulate any nonverbal component if it has a good reason to do so. He explained further:

> [A] government regulation is sufficiently justified if it is within the constitutional power of the government; if it furthers an important or substantial governmental interest; if the governmental interest is unrelated to the suppression of free expression; and if the incidental restriction on alleged First Amendment freedoms is no greater than is essential to the furtherance of that interest.

Let's break this down a little. What Chief Justice Warren was saying is that in order for the regulation to stay on the good side of the First Amendment it needs to clear four prongs. First, the government must have the constitutional power to pass the regulation (no shocker here); second, the regulation must further an "important" or "substantial" government interest; third, the interest cannot be related to restricting free expression; and fourth, it must restrict no more speech than is needed to further that interest (here again, the tricky narrow-tailoring requirement). The O'Brien Test isn't quite strict scrutiny, but it's not rational basis review either. The test falls somewhere in the middle, leading imaginative lawyers to give it the name "intermediate scrutiny."

Now that we have our standard, let's see how the Supreme Court applied it to the facts of the case. The government was not limiting verbal advocacy directed against the draft, only to the action of destroying draft cards. The first prong of the test is satisfied because Congress has the constitutional power to raise armies. The second prong is satisfied as well because the government has a substantial interest in maintaining a functioning draft system and the law criminalizing the destruction of draft cards furthers that interest. The third prong is less clear. O'Brien argued that Congress passed the law in order to suppress free expression and shut down those who opposed the war in Vietnam. The Court rejected this argument because "inquiries into congressional motives or purposes are a hazardous manner." In general, courts try to avoid reading the minds of representatives and senators to discern "an alleged illicit legislative motive" behind otherwise constitutional legislation. Finally, they concluded that the fourth prong was satisfied because the federal statute only prohibited destroying draft cards and left open "ample alternative channels" for those who opposed the draft to express their views. Accordingly, they upheld O'Brien's conviction.

A good counterpoint to *O'Brien* is the case of *Tinker v. Des Moines Independent Community School District* (1969). A group of middle and high school students in Des Moines, Iowa, decided in the winter of 1965 to express their objections to the Vietnam War by wearing black armbands to class. School administrators had gotten wind of the protest and announced a policy two days beforehand that any students found wearing black armbands would be asked to remove them or face suspension. The children went to school wearing the armbands anyway, refused to take them off, and were suspended. With the help of the ACLU, the families sued in federal court to overturn the decision of the school board, and the case eventually ended up in front of the Supreme Court.

A 7–2 majority voted to overturn the decision of the Des Moines school board, finding that while students do not have unlimited free speech rights in school, they also do not "shed their constitutional rights to freedom of speech or expression at the schoolhouse gate." The question was whether by wearing black armbands the protestors were "materially and substantially interfer[ing] with the requirements of appropriate discipline in the operation of the school." Justice Abe Fortas, writing for the majority, held that it did not. Furthermore, the banning of black armbands was not part of a broader dress code to keep political symbols out of school, since the record showed that "some of the students wore buttons relating to national political campaigns, and some even wore the Iron Cross, traditionally a symbol of Nazism." The majority was clear: school officials may not ban symbolic speech based on mere "undifferentiated fear or apprehension of disturbance."

Justice Black, usually a First Amendment absolutist, issued a strongly worded dissent: "If the time has come when pupils of state-supported schools . . . can defy and flout orders of school officials to keep their minds on their own schoolwork, it is the beginning of a new revolutionary era of permissiveness in this country fostered by the judiciary."

Let's tackle another popular symbolic speech issue: flag burning. The first time the U.S. Supreme Court addressed the issue of flag burning was in *Street v. New York* (1969). A New York City resident had been arrested, tried, and convicted for burning a flag as an act of protest, in violation of state law. The Supreme Court overturned his conviction on free speech grounds but did not address whether flag burning itself was protected. Five years later in *Spence v. Washington* (1974), a six-justice majority overturned the flag mutilation conviction of a man who had displayed the American flag with a peace sign taped on it in protest of the Vietnam War and Kent State shootings. Three dissenting justices argued that the government has the constitutional authority to protect the flag as a "symbol of nationhood and unity."

Unlike the many areas of the First Amendment covered in this book that are still left unsettled, the flag burning question received a definite answer in the 1989 case of *Texas v. Johnson*. Gregory Lee Johnson, a member of the Revolutionary Communist Youth Brigade, was arrested, tried, and convicted of violating a Texas statute when he burned the American flag during a demonstration in front of the

1984 Republican National Convention in Dallas. A fiercely divided Supreme Court overturned his conviction by a 5–4 margin. Justice William Brennan wrote a lengthy majority opinion that analyzed the constitutionality of flag burning from nearly every conceivable angle— serendipitously providing a great overview for us!

He began by recognizing that even though burning a flag is conduct, its "expressive, overtly political nature" includes it in the category of symbolic speech worthy of First Amendment protection. His next step was to determine whether the Court should apply the O'Brien Test to the Texas statute. Justice Brennan noted that the O'Brien Test applies only in cases where "the governmental interest is unrelated to the suppression of free expression." Texas offered two interests to justify the statute: "preventing breaches of the peace, and preserving the flag as a symbol of nationhood and national unity." The first reason sounds like a claim of First Amendment exception under "incitement" from *Brandenburg v. Ohio* or "fighting words" from *Chaplinsky v. New Hampshire,* so Brennan analyzed it under both. Remember that the *Brandenburg* test requires both intent and likelihood that the speech will "incite or produce imminent lawless action" in order to criminalize it. There was no evidence of either in this case, so the majority refused to accept Texas's argument that every instance of flag burning carries with it the "potential for a breach of the peace." Nor does this justification qualify for the fighting words exception, since "no reasonable onlooker would have regarded [Johnson's] general dissatisfaction with the policies of the Federal Government as a direct personal insult or an invitation to exchange fisticuffs." Since preventing breaches of the peace was not a permissible reason for banning flag burning, and since the desire to preserve the flag as a symbol by criminalizing its destruction was entirely related to suppressing freedom of expression, the majority concluded: "We are thus outside of *O'Brien's* test altogether."

The majority opinion now got down to the real question it needed to answer: Even though flag burning is speech, should the government nevertheless have the power to protect it against destruction or mutilation? In other words, should flag burning qualify for one of the First Amendment exceptions? The majority concluded that there is "no indication—either in the text of the Constitution or in our cases interpreting it—that a separate juridical category exists for the American flag alone," and they declined "to create for the flag an exception to the just principles protected by the First Amendment." If the government could criminalize flag burning, where should the Court draw the line? "Could the government, on this theory, prohibit the burning of state flags? How about copies of the Presidential Seal? Or the Constitution?" The majority decided that the better course of action would be to stick with the "bedrock principle underlying the First Amendment . . . that the Government may not prohibit the expression of an idea simply because society finds the idea itself offensive or disagreeable."

Chief Justice Rehnquist and the three other dissenters argued that the flag deserves special protection as a national symbol and that burning it publicly should at least be treated as fighting words, since it is done "not to express any particular idea, but to antagonize others." The raw emotions surrounding this subject are evident in the tone of their dissent. Rehnquist excoriated the majority for overturning the anti-flag burning laws of the federal government and 48 of the 50 states, and for taking on the "role [of] a platonic guardian admonishing those responsible to public opinion as if they were truant school children."

The backlash against the Supreme Court's decision in *Texas v. Johnson* was swift and immediate. Large majorities in both the House and Senate passed the Flag Protection Act of 1989, which was signed into law by President George H.W. Bush. No sooner did the bill become law than Gregory Lee Johnson violated it by burning a flag once again.

The Supreme Court took up his case, along with those of several other defendants, in *United States v. Eichman* (1990). In perhaps the biggest non-surprise ever, the justices lined up exactly as they did the year before and voted 5–4 to overturn the new law for violating the First Amendment.

Postscript: For the next sixteen years, every Congress attempted to pass a flag desecration amendment to the U.S. Constitution that would overturn the Supreme Court's decisions. In 2006, the measure fell one vote shy in the Senate of being sent to the states for ratification. Unless the constitutional amendment passes or the Supreme Court decides to reverse *Texas v. Johnson*, burning the flag is protected speech under the First Amendment.

The final area of symbolic speech we will cover here ties in nicely with our discussion of hate speech from the last chapter. The Supreme Court might still be wrestling with how to handle speech that directly maligns members of a group, but what about the ultimate act of symbolic hate speech: cross burning? This is the question the justices were asked to take up in the 1992 case of *R.A.V. v. City of St. Paul*.

In the early morning hours of June 21, 1990, a group of teenagers burned a wooden cross on the front lawn of a black family in St. Paul, MN. The youths were arrested and charged with violating the St. Paul Bias-Motivated Crime Ordinance, which read:

*Whoever places on public or private property, a symbol, object, appellation, characterization or graffiti, including, but not limited to, a burning cross or Nazi swastika, which one knows or has reasonable grounds to know arouses anger, alarm or resentment in others on the basis of race, color, creed, religion or gender commits disorderly conduct and shall be guilty of a misdemeanor.*

The teenagers appealed the charge up to the U.S. Supreme Court, resulting in one of the most fractious unanimous decisions that body has ever produced. All nine justices agreed that the St. Paul Ordinance was unconstitutional, but four of them disagreed strongly with the majority's reasoning. The five-justice majority opinion, written by Justice Scalia, sought to redefine the categorical exclusions to the First Amendment from *Chaplinksy.* According to the majority, the excluded forms of speech from *Chaplinksy,* such as fighting words, obscenity, and libel, are not "entirely invisible to the Constitution." When the government regulates fighting words, they argued, what it really is doing is regulating the "'nonspeech' element of communication . . . analogous to a noisy sound truck." The problem the majority had with the St. Paul Ordinance was that even though it sought to proscribe certain types of symbolic speech as fighting words, the measure applied only to words that related to "specified, disfavored topics"— namely, race, religion, and gender, not such other ideas as "political affiliation, union membership, or homosexuality." In other words, because the ordinance was aimed at suppressing speech having to do with "favored topics," it was an impermissible content-based restriction on speech.

Three of the four concurring justices disagreed so strongly with the majority's reasoning that they wrote separate opinions of their own. The most important came from Justice Stevens, who outlined "a rough hierarchy in the constitutional protection of speech":

*Core political speech occupies the highest, most protected position; commercial speech and non-obscene, sexually explicit speech are regarded as a sort of second-class expression; obscenity and fighting words receive the least protection of all.*

In this case, he argued, the ordinance prohibited "only low-value speech, namely, fighting words" and regulated only "expressive conduct [rather] than . . . the written or spoken word." Justice Stevens also emphasized that the act of cross burning in this case "was nothing more than a crude form of physical intimidation" and had been intended "by its very [execution to] inflict injury." He had absolutely no problem with the fact that the St. Paul ordinance was content-based; the problem was that it was overbroad.

Justice Stevens would see his view partially vindicated a decade later in *Virginia v. Black* (2003), another cross burning case. This one dealt with a challenge to a Virginia statute that made it a crime to burn a cross "with the intent of intimidating any person or group of persons." The law also included this provision: "Any such burning of a cross shall be prima facie evidence of an intent to intimidate a person or group of persons." (Prima facie evidence is a legal term that means the evidence is sufficient to prove the case, unless it is otherwise rebutted or disproven.) Essentially, what the statute did was make cross burning with the intent to intimidate a crime, while also saying that the act of cross burning itself displays intent to intimidate. It thereby shifted the burden to the defendant to prove otherwise. This is where the statute ran into trouble at the Supreme Court.

No single opinion was able to command a majority of the justices in this case, but five of them did agree that the Virginia statute violated the First Amendment. The plurality opinion, written by Justice O'Connor, stressed that "true threats" are indeed one of the exemptions to the First Amendment. The true threats doctrine—first established in the 1969 case of *Watts v. United States,* in which the Court ruled that the government could criminalize threats to assassinate the president—excludes from First Amendment protection "statements where the speaker means to communicate a serious expression of an intent to commit an act of unlawful violence to a particular individual or group of individuals." The plurality in *Virginia v. Black* also held that the statute complied with *R.A.V.* because it banned all threats to intimidate, without limitation.

The problem was that pesky prima facie evidence provision. Not only did it functionally erase the "intent to intimidate" requirement by saying that all cross burnings are designed to intimidate, but it also unconstitutionally shifted the burden onto the defendant in a criminal case to disprove his intent. Justice Thomas dissented, arguing that the history of cross burning in the United States is so closely tied to anti-black terrorism that it should be categorically excluded from the First Amendment under *Chaplinksy.* Justices Souter, Ginsburg, and Kennedy dissented, on the other hand, because they believed that cross burning is constitutionally protected symbolic speech and the Virginia statute made a content-based distinction in violation of *R.A.V.*

The takeaway from this case is that a state may criminalize cross burning as long as it does so for the purpose of preventing intimidation and doesn't shift the burden of proof onto the defendant.

# ✦ 13 ✦

## I KNOW IT WHEN I SEE IT: OBSCENITY LAW AND POLITICAL SPEECH SINCE THE AGE OF AQUARIUS

O K, AFTER ALL THAT TALK ABOUT FIGHTING WORDS, hate speech, burning things, and other *Chaplinsky* exceptions to free speech rights, let's have a look at obscenity. Wait, that didn't come out right!

Obscenity is another one of those "categorical" exceptions to the First Amendment that isn't quite so categorical. Even if we accept the premise that obscene material is not deserving of First Amendment protection, how do we determine what qualifies as obscene? After all, what's obscene to one person might be perfectly fine to another. Given that tastes and individual morality are so different, what objective standard can we use to determine when merely objectionable speech crosses the line into impermissible obscenity? Is it possible to draw any meaningful distinction here, or will such determinations always be subjective?

Regardless of how you answer those questions, obscenity regulation had existed in the United States long before the Supreme Court recognized it as an exception to the First Amendment in *Chaplinsky*. Although pornography has existed for thousands of years, it occupied a legal gray zone for most of modern Western history. Like prostitution, it was often technically illegal but tolerated and remained mostly a small-scale, underground activity. The simultaneous growth of the photography, shipping, and publication industries in the second half of the 19th century led to the first major boom in pornography as a business. This coincided with the transformation of adult products such as contraceptives and sex toys from handmade, artisanal creations into mass-produced commercialized goods. Even abortion providers were beginning to advertise openly. All of these developments created a kind of moral panic that led, not surprisingly, to laws attempting to put the sexual genie back in the bottle. In 1873, Congress passed an extensive

series of measures called the Comstock Law that made it a federal crime to circulate erotica, contraceptives, sex toys, and even personal letters containing salacious content through the mail. Many states also cracked down on obscenity by passing laws that criminalized even the personal possession of such items.

The extent of early U.S. anti-obscenity regulation is shocking and mostly forgotten in the modern day. Postal inspectors had nearly unlimited power to read through people's mail and ban anything they considered obscene. And prosecutors were not shy about using the law to punish recalcitrant offenders. Publisher H. L. Mencken was arrested and fined for distributing copies of his satirical magazine the *American Mercury*, and the Broadway play *Sex* was shut down and actress Mae West imprisoned for ten days because it was deemed obscene. Birth control pioneer Margaret Sanger and several others were either fined or jailed for distributing sex education literature and information on birth control. Even some anatomy textbooks were banned for depicting supposedly obscene material.

The Supreme Court sidestepped First Amendment challenges to anti-obscenity legislation prior to the 1950s. There had been a few sporadic victories for free speech proponents— as in 1933, when a federal court

in New York overturned the obscenity ban on importing copies of James Joyce's novel *Ulysses*—but in general the courts took a hands-off approach. The first time the Supreme Court examined the constitutionality of these laws was in the case of *Roth v. United States* (1957). Roth was a New York publisher who had been convicted of distributing copies of his pornographic magazine, *American Aphrodite*, through the mail, in violation of state and federal law. The six-justice majority opinion, written by Justice Brennan, noted that while "obscenity is not within the area of constitutionally protected speech or press,"

> *sex and obscenity are not synonymous. . . . The portrayal of sex, e.g., in art, literature, and scientific words, is not itself sufficient reason to deny material the constitutional protection of freedom of speech and press.*

The dividing line for the Supreme Court between constitutionally protected sex speech and obscenity is whether the work was designed to "appeal to the prurient interest." This awkward phrase is the language the Court used in *Roth*, though Justice Brennan seemed to understand that it would elicit raised eyebrows and confused expressions so included a lengthy definition in a footnote. Something appealing to the prurient interest means it is intended to "excite lustful thoughts"; encourage "itching, morbid, or lascivious longings"; or promote "a shameful or morbid interest in nudity, sex, or excretion . . . [that] goes substantially beyond customary limits of candor in description or representation of such matters."

The traditional common law rule of obscenity came from the English case of *Regina v. Hicklin*, which asked whether the material tended "to deprave and corrupt those whose minds are open to such immoral influences." The majority in *Roth*, however, believed that the *Hicklin* test was too broad and devised a new one. Its new test would ask the jury to determine

whether to the average person, applying contemporary community standards, the dominant theme of the material taken as a whole appeals to the prurient interest.

The Court upheld Roth's conviction since his magazine failed this new test. Justices Douglas and Black dissented, as they did in every case dealing with a restriction on speech, because they believed that the First Amendment protects all forms of speech absolutely, obscenity included.

While it might not sound like it at first, the *Roth* ruling was actually a big shift. What is and is not obscene would no longer be determined by the personal morality of elderly, black-robed gentlemen sitting on the judge's bench, but by the average person applying contemporary community standards. Moreover, an isolated use of obscenity, like an explicit description of sex in an otherwise nonsexual novel, would not render the entire book obscene if did not represent the "dominant theme" of the work. Yet the Roth Test still had a lot of holes. For instance, what "community" did they mean? Was it the local community, the national community, or even the world community? And how can you determine the standards of an entire community?

If you think these questions are hard, so did the Supreme Court. The justices had a tough time figuring out how to apply the new Roth Test in the rapidly changing social atmosphere of the 1960s "sexual revolution." Every member adopted his own take on the Roth Test, leading to fractured decisions where no opinion could command a majority of the justices. For example, they upheld bans on "hard core" pornography in movie theaters while never being able to agree on exactly what hard core pornography is. Most famously, in the case of *Jacobellis v. Ohio* (1966), they overturned the obscenity conviction of a theater owner for showing the French film *Les Amants;* Justice Potter Stewart, concurring, offered the priceless statement:

> *I shall not today attempt further to define the kinds of material I understand to be embraced within that shorthand description [of hard core pornography]; and perhaps I could never succeed in intelligibly doing so.* **But I know it when I see it**, *and the motion picture involved in this case is not that.*
> [Emphasis added]

The situation got so bad that the Court stopped issuing useless written decisions that contained six or seven different opinions, and it began ordering the reversal of obscenity convictions when at least five justices, applying separate tests, determined that the regulation violated the First Amendment.

The justices finally reached a breakthrough at the end of the decade in the case of *Stanley v. Georgia* (1969). The police had obtained a warrant to search a home for illegal bookmaking materials and instead found several reels of film containing pornographic movies. The defendant was arrested, charged, and convicted of possessing obscene material in violation of Georgia law. A unanimous U.S. Supreme Court voted to overturn the conviction, with five justices agreeing on a single majority opinion for the first time in memory.

Justice Marshall, writing the opinion of the Court, drew a sharp distinction between cases dealing with "public" displays of obscenity and those dealing with the private possession of obscene material, at issue in this instance. In recent years, the Court had recognized that the Constitution guarantees "the right to be free, except in very limited circumstances, from unwanted governmental intrusions into one's privacy." This implicit constitutional right to privacy would later be used to overturn abortion bans in *Roe v. Wade* (1973), but here it formed the foundation of the Court's ruling on the possession of obscene materials:

> *If the First Amendment means anything, it means that a State has no business telling a man, sitting alone in his own house, what books he may read or what films he may watch.*

The home is a private, protected space where state power must give way to "the individual's right to read or observe what he pleases."

The Court refused to extend the holding of *Stanley* to areas beyond private possession. Its landmark decision in *Miller v. California* (1973), finally attempted to put the question of public obscenity to rest and provide clear direction to lower courts—with mixed results. A 5–4 majority voted to uphold a conviction for sending sexually explicit brochures through the mail and agreed on a single test to use in public obscenity cases. From now on, in addition to the Roth Test ("whether the average person, applying contemporary community standards, would find that the dominant theme of the work, taken as a whole, appeals to the prurient interest") the jury would also need to determine "whether the work depicts or describes, in a patently offensive way, sexual conduct specifically defined by the applicable state law" and "whether the work, taken as a whole, lacks serious literary, artistic, political, or scientific value."

The majority also settled the question of what "contemporary community standards" means by employing a blatant contradiction in terms. Its opinion began with a straightforward declaration: "Under a National Constitution, fundamental First Amendment limitations on the powers of the States do not vary from community to community." However, it went on,

*this does not mean that there are, or should or can be, fixed, uniform national standards of precisely what appeals to the "prurient interest" or is "patently offensive."*

Yes, you read that right. The First Amendment applies equally throughout the country, but the standard for what it protects varies from community to community. According to the majority, "our nation is simply too big and diverse for this Court to reasonably expect that such standards could be articulated for all 50 States in a single formulation." Because it is "neither realistic nor constitutionally sound to read the First Amendment as requiring that the people of Maine or Mississippi accept public depiction of conduct found tolerable in Las Vegas or New York City," the majority refused to "strangle" the diversity of "tastes and attitudes" with "the absolutism of imposed uniformity." Therefore, the jury in obscenity cases will be asked to apply the standards of the local community and not a uniform, national standard.

Decided on the same day as *Miller* was another key obscenity case, *Paris Adult Theatre I v. Slaton* (1973). Here, a 5–4 majority applied the Miller Test and upheld a Georgia statute that banned the screening of pornographic films in places of "public accommodation" such as movie theaters. Justice Brennan, the author of the Roth Test, had by now abandoned his creation and dissented in both *Miller* and *Slaton*. In his *Paris* dissent, joined by Justices Stewart and Marshall, he lamented the Supreme Court's failure to provide the "sensitive tools" needed to separate obscenity from "other sexually oriented but constitutionally protected speech." Although the dissenters recognized that the government has a legitimate interest in regulating "the morality of the community," they believed that "these interests cannot justify the substantial damage to constitutional rights and to this Nation's judicial machinery that inevitably results from state efforts to bar the distribution of [sexually explicit] material to consenting adults." Except when it came to protecting juveniles or nonconsenting adults, the dissenters would have prohibited the government "from attempting wholly to suppress sexually oriented materials on the basis of their allegedly 'obscene' contents."

For all the confusion swirling around the constitutional status of adult pornography, the U.S. Supreme Court has consistently held that the First Amendment does not protect child pornography. In *New York v. Ferber* (1982), all nine justices voted to uphold a New York statute that made it a crime to distribute sexually explicit material involving a child less than sixteen years old. Justice White, writing the majority opinion, included child pornography as one of the categorical exclusions from the First Amendment. The Court did not need to apply the Miller Test because child pornography is unprotected speech regardless of whether it qualifies as obscene under *Miller*. This is based on the fact that the government has a compelling interest in protecting children from the physical, psychological, and sexual exploitation that inevitably results from the creation of child pornography.

Nor is the mere possession of child pornography constitutionally protected. In *Osborne v. Ohio* (1990), a six-justice majority refused to extend the holding of *Stanley*, that an individual has the right "to read or observe what he pleases" in his own home, to the realm of child pornography. The key point both here and in *Ferber* is not that the government has a "paternalistic interest" in stamping out a deviant sexual fetish, but that it has a compelling interest in protecting the well-being of minors.

Under the same reasoning, however, the Supreme Court in *Ashcroft v. Free Speech Coalition* (2002) struck down a portion of the Child Pornography Prevention Act of 1996 that banned "virtual" child pornography. No actual children are harmed in the creation of computer-simulated child pornography or scenarios where adults act as underage children. The law in question had not been designed to protect real children from abuse, but rather to ban virtual child porn because it is, in a word, icky. And that is something the First Amendment will not allow. As the Court held in *Ashcroft*, the government "cannot constitutionally premise legislation on the desirability of controlling a person's private thoughts."

Given that the Supreme Court has recognized a compelling state interest in protecting children from harm—how far does that go? Can the government criminalize indecent but not obscene speech that might reach the ears of minors? The Court was asked to take up this issue in *Federal Communications Commission v. Pacifica Foundation* (1978). The FCC had received a complaint from a father who had been driving in the car with his young son when a New York radio station aired comedian George Carlin's twelve-minute monologue, "Seven Words

You Can Never Say on Television." (Go ahead, Google it now!) The FCC sanctioned the radio station for violating its indecency regulations and warned that any further violations would result in fines or the suspension of its broadcast license. The Supreme Court had ruled previously in *Ginsberg v. New York* (1968) that the government could prohibit the sale of indecent, but not obscene material to minors. Should this rule apply to broadcasts as well?

A five-justice majority in *Pacifica* said yes and voted to uphold the FCC's actions, finding that the government has the power to regulate broadcast indecent language, even if the language is not obscene under the Miller Test. The majority based its decision on both the government's interest in protecting children and the "uniquely pervasive presence" of broadcast media.

*Patently offensive, indecent material presented over the airwaves confronts the citizen, not only in public, but also in the privacy of the home, where the individual's right to be let alone plainly outweighs the First Amendment rights of an intruder.*

Also at play in this case was a TPM component of broadcast regulation. The airwaves are public property but do not qualify as a traditional public forum. Since the government owns the airwaves and licenses their use to commercial broadcasters, they are able to set certain restrictions on its use.

This issue returned more recently as the FCC stepped up pressure on broadcasters in the wake of the Janet Jackson–Justin Timberlake "wardrobe malfunction" incident during the Super Bowl XXXVIII halftime show in 2004. Fines for indecency violations increased from $27,500 to $325,000 per incident, and even single, unscripted uses of profanity (so-called "fleeting expletives") now would be treated as violations. The FCC attempted to levy such fines on Fox Television after Cher and Nicole Richie dropped F-bombs during the network's Billboard Music Awards in 2002 and 2003, resulting in protracted litigation. In *Federal Communications Commission v. Fox Television Stations, Inc.* (2012), the Court overturned the FCC regulation for being unconstitutionally vague and invalidated the fines, but it dodged the larger First Amendment question of whether such a draconian rule is permissible at all.

However, the Supreme Court has refused to extend the holdings of *Pacifica* and *Ginsberg* to allow the government to restrict the sale of violent video games to minors. In *Brown v. Entertainment Merchants Association* (2011), a 7–2 majority voted to strike down a California law that made the sale or rental of violent video games to minors punishable by a $1,000 fine. Although California attempted to shore up the constitutionality of the law by having it apply only to violent video games that fail the Miller Test, that wasn't enough for Justice Scalia, writing the majority opinion:

*California has tried to make violent-speech regulation look like obscenity regulation . . . [but our] cases have been clear that the obscenity exception to the First Amendment does not cover whatever a legislature finds shocking, but only depictions of 'sexual conduct.' . . . Speech about violence is not obscene."*

So in case you had any questions about permissibility standards in American law, there it is, straight from the Supreme Court's mouth:

- depictions of sexual content—possibly obscene under *Miller* and subject to criminal penalties including fines and imprisonment.
- depictions of violence, no matter how graphic and targeted at children— absolutely protected under the First Amendment.

How about sexual content on the Internet? Can the government regulate such material to protect children? The growth of the Internet in the 1990s created a new moral panic as adults learned how easy it was for tech-savvy minors to access grainy, pixelated photographs of nude models and worse. Congress responded by passing the Communications Decency Act of 1996 (CDA), which included a provision criminalizing the knowing transmission of obscene, indecent, or "patently offensive" materials to anyone under the age of 18.

In *Reno v. American Civil Liberties Union* (1997), the Supreme Court struck down this provision as a bridge too far. The Internet—which they analogized to "a series of tubes" (no, just joking, they didn't actually say that!)—is a very different beast from either radio or television. Unlike broadcast media, the justices recognized, "the receipt of information on the Internet requires a series of affirmative steps more deliberate and directed than merely turning a dial." They also found that Internet users "seldom encounter content 'by accident.'" The CDA impermissibly criminalized "a large amount of speech that adults have a constitutional right to receive and to address to one another" in order to deny minors access to that material. In an interesting separate opinion, Justice O'Connor analyzed the CDA through the lens of a zoning law that had attempted to carve out "adult zones" on the Internet. Restricting certain content to verifiably adult-only zones would be constitutionally permissible in theory, but admittedly impossible on "the Internet as it exists in 1997."

Undeterred by the Supreme Court striking down the CDA, Congress tried again to regulate Internet pornography by passing the Child Online Protection Act (COPA) in 1998. The legislators hoped it would be more palatable to the Court by restricting only material that is displayed on the World Wide Web (as opposed to private communications via chat rooms and email) for "commercial purposes"; that is obscene as defined by the Miller Test; and that is available to minors. As expected, the COPA faced immediate court challenges.

An eight-justice majority in *Ashcroft v. American Civil Liberties Union* (2002) decided to leave in place a Circuit Court injunction of the COPA, effectively blocking the law from going into effect. The most interesting part of their decision was a lengthy and fractured debate over how to apply the "community standards" prong of the Miller Test to material distributed over the Internet. The Court might have been able to sweep the monster of predicating First Amendment rights on variable local standards under the rug back in the 1970s, but the worldwide reach of the Internet exposed

the contradictions of such an approach. Inherent in the medium is a paradox that makes it unique from every other form of communication in human history. As a lower court ruling put it, the Internet "is easy and cheap to reach a worldwide

audience . . . but expensive if not impossible to reach a geographic subset." This means that disseminators of information, even if they want to, cannot prohibit their material from going to places where it might be considered obscene based on local community standards. In the words of Justice Breyer, this "subjects every Internet speaker to the standards of the most puritanical community in the United States," allowing them to exercise "a heckler's Internet veto affecting the rest of the Nation."

In spite of these concerns, only Justice Stevens urged a wholesale reexamination, noting that "in the context of the Internet . . . community standards become a sword, rather than a shield." Justice Thomas, writing the majority opinion, waved aside that issue: "It is sufficient to note that community standards need not be defined by reference to a precise geographic area. . . . [We] do not believe that the medium's 'unique characteristics' justify adopting a different approach." Justice O'Connor, in a separate concurrence, advocated "adopting a national standard for obscenity for regulation of the Internet."

Where does all this leave obscenity jurisprudence? The vague Miller Test, with its variable community standards prong, is still controlling, but it is so riddled with exceptions and contradictions that it is less stable than ever. Of all the *Chaplinksy* exceptions to the First Amendment, obscenity had always been the most problematic. As of 2017, the obscenity exception was limited only to certain types of sexual content and no other forms of graphic speech. It appears, for the time being, that the Supreme Court will continue to apply *Miller's* localized community standards test to obscenity regulation even as the Internet exposes that standard as increasingly unworkable. At the same time, the undeniable trajectory of the Court's decisions over the past several decades has been to expand First Amendment protections and restrict exceptions to a few narrowly defined areas that are treated almost like grandfather clauses. We will examine the last of these *Chaplinksy* exceptions in the next chapter.

# ✦ 14 ✦

## DON'T DEFAME ME, BRO!

**U**P TO NOW, ALL OUR DISCUSSIONS OF FREE SPEECH have had to do with government attempts to regulate, limit, or shut it down in some way. This makes sense, since we learned way back in Chapter 2 that the Constitution applies only to state, rather than individual, action. However, there is one semi-exception to this where the First Amendment does apply to the actions of individuals: civil lawsuits having to do with **defamation** and the intentional infliction of emotional distress.

# CRIMINAL LAW VS. CIVIL LAW

In **criminal law**, the government prohibits certain behavior by imposing penalties on violators. Such behavior runs the gamut from minor offenses like jaywalking to capital offenses like murder, but the penalty is always the loss of some fundamental right. This might be loss of the right to property through fines or confiscation; loss of the right to liberty through imprisonment, travel, or living restrictions; or even, most controversially, loss of the right to life through the imposition of the death penalty. In order to strip a person of these rights, the government must first jump through a number of constitutional hoops by providing notice of the law, the right to an attorney, the right to a speedy trial, the right to a trial by jury, the right against self-incrimination, and an overall fair trial in which the prosecution must prove every element of the crime beyond a reasonable doubt. The theory behind criminal law is that individuals who violate these rules are harming the public as a whole and the government is punishing them on the public's behalf. This is why criminal prosecutions in the United States are done on behalf of "The State" or "The People."

**Civil law**, on the other hand, deals with private disputes. Think of all the different types of lawsuits you have heard about: breach of contract, medical malpractice, battery, etc. Any time one party sues another party, we're squarely in the realm of civil law. The purpose of a civil suit is not to punish, but rather to "make the injured party whole" by having the offender pay compensation for any damages they caused. A civil wrong is called a **tort**. Defamation is one of them.

CRIMINAL LAW

CIVIL LAW

Because defamation came out of the common law rather than statute, the question of what exactly qualifies varies widely throughout the country. In general, defamation falls into two broad categories: **written defamation, known as libel,** and **verbal defamation, known as slander.** To meet the legal definition, both libel and slander must cause damage to a person's reputation and must be untrue. Some states still follow an old common law rule that views certain statements as being so vile, so beyond the pale—such as "imputing unchastity to a woman," claiming that a person suffers from a venereal disease, or that he or she engages in sodomy—that the plaintiff (the person bringing the lawsuit) does not even need to prove that their reputation was actually damaged in order to prevail! In spite of these strange Victorian holdovers, the vast majority of defamation cases have to do with untrue, damaging statements about another's business practices or accusations that they committed a crime.

So where does the First Amendment fit in with all this? Although the First Amendment never applies to private activity, a lawsuit by one person against another brings the state into the equation. The government, through the judicial machinery of the courts, can exercise coercive power either by forbidding a person from speaking (by issuing an injunction) or by forcing them to pay money to another person because of their damaging speech. If you recall, libel was one of the "categorical exclusions" from the First Amendment listed in *Chaplinsky*, and the Supreme Court upheld a criminal "group libel" law in *Beauharnais*. Does this mean that civil libel falls outside the realm of constitutional speech? Fortunately, unlike other areas of the First Amendment, there is one definitive rule that applies here. It comes from the landmark 1964 case of *New York Times Co. v. Sullivan*.

The incorporation of the First Amendment to the states meant that undesirable speech could no longer be criminalized. As the Civil Rights movement heated up in the 1960s, a number of Southern states sought other methods to shut it down. Since the criminal law was off the table, some public officials in these states decided that they would use the civil law to accomplish the same goals. They began suing organizations that ran stories critical of their segregationist policies for libel. By all accounts, this was a highly effective tactic. Southern officials won millions of dollars in damage awards from these suits, and the legal risk made all but the largest publishers shy away from printing such stories.

In 1960, a civil rights group ran a full-page ad in the *New York Times* that criticized the "unprecedented wave of terror" employed by the

Montgomery, Alabama, police against demonstrators. The ad claimed that the police had repeatedly assaulted Dr. Martin Luther King, Jr. and arrested him on seven separate occasions. Although he was not mentioned by name, L.B. Sullivan, the Montgomery police commissioner, sued the newspaper for libel. Alabama had very loose libel laws, allowing a plaintiff to recover damages if he could prove that the words "would tend to injure [his] reputation" or to "bring [him] into public contempt." The plaintiff did not need to prove that he suffered any actual damages, and the only defense was to prove that all the words spoken or printed were true. Because some of the claims contained in the ad were exaggerated (e.g., Dr. King had been arrested in Montgomery only four times rather than seven), Sullivan prevailed and won a judgement of $500,000. *The New York Times* promptly appealed the case to the Supreme Court.

A unanimous Supreme Court voted to overturn the judgement, with the majority announcing a new way forward on libel cases. The problem here was obvious: public officials were using libel suits as an end-around to restrict freedom of speech. As Justice Brennan wrote in the majority opinion, "what a State may not constitutionally bring about by means of a criminal statute is likewise beyond the reach of its civil law of libel." The simple fact that some of the claims were untrue had no impact on First Amendment status since "constitutional protection does not turn upon the truth, popularity, or social utility of the ideas and beliefs which are offered." Justice Brennan analogized the case to the 1798 Alien and Sedition Acts:

*Although the Sedition Act was never tested in this Court, the attack upon its validity has carried the day in the court of history. . . . These criticisms reflect a broad consensus that the Act, because of the restraint it imposed upon criticism of government and public officials, was inconsistent with the First Amendment.*

Thus, public officials were forbidden from using libel suits to intimidate their critics into silence. From this point on, in order to prevail in a defamation lawsuit, a public official would need to prove that the statement was made with "actual malice," meaning "with knowledge that it was false or with reckless disregard of whether it was false or not."

The question left hanging after *Sullivan* was how far the Supreme Court would go in extending First Amendment protection in defamation cases. Public officials would have to pass the Sullivan Test in order to win a defamation suit, but what about nongovernmental "public figures," such as media personalities, sports stars, and other celebrities? Should speech concerning them also receive a heightened degree of constitutional protection?

*Curtis Publishing Co. v. Butts* (1967) was the first test of whether the Court would extend the Sullivan Test to people other than public officials. The *Saturday Evening Post* ran a story in which the authors claimed that Wally Butts, the University of Georgia football coach, and Bear Bryant, the University of Alabama football coach, had conspired to fix games. The reporting was done with, to put it lightly, shoddy investigative standards based on uncorroborated statements and little fact checking. The coaches sued the magazine for libel, and the jury returned a multimillion-dollar verdict. The magazine appealed to the Supreme Court, arguing that the article should receive First Amendment protection under *Sullivan* since it was reporting on public figures.

A majority of the Court held that speech regarding public figures should receive the same degree of constitutional protection as speech about public officials. As stated by Chief Justice Earl Warren, "differentiation between 'public figures' and 'public officials' and adoption of separate standards of proof for each have no basis in law, logic, or First Amendment policy." Even though public figures do not occupy formal positions of government power, Warren wrote, they "often play an influential role in ordering society." Because of this, he concluded,

> *Our citizenry has a legitimate and substantial interest in the conduct of such persons, and freedom of the press to engage in uninhibited debate about their involvement in public issues and events is as crucial as it is in the case of "public officials."*

And the majority in *Curtis* noted another important connection between public officials and public figures, also separating them from private figures: Public figures have "ready access . . . to mass media of communication, both to influence policy and to counter criticism of their views and activities." In short, the First Amendment should protect speech regarding public figures no less than public officials both because they operate in the public arena and because they have access to rebuttal tools that the average person does not have. Public figures can defend themselves from bad speech by appearing on the news, issuing a press release, sitting for an interview, or now blasting out a few tweets to present their side of the story to an audience of millions.

Chief Justice Earl Warren

As it turned out, despite extending the Sullivan Test to public figures, the Court in *Curtis* still upheld the libel judgement. The reporting of the *Saturday Evening Post* was found to be so bad, with so little basis in fact, that it displayed "actual malice" by exhibiting "reckless disregard for the truth." The First Amendment might be a shield, but it is not an impenetrable one. Outright lies or complete fabrications written about public figures can still result in a libel judgement.

Continuing down the rabbit hole . . . Exactly how do you differentiate between public figures and private figures? The Supreme Court has never created a definitive test to determine this, but its rulings have tended to construe the "public figures" category rather narrowly. They have determined that well-known attorneys, wealthy socialites, scientists receiving large grants, and individuals who make a brief appearance in the news are not considered public figures for First Amendment purposes. Factors the justices will look at in determining public figure status are whether the person has achieved "general fame or notoriety in the community [or] pervasive involvement in the affairs of society"; if they have assumed "any role of special prominence in the affairs of society"; and if they have "voluntarily thrust" or "injected" themselves into the public sphere in order to "influence others."

The other big area of civil law that bumps up against First Amendment freedom of speech has to do with lawsuits claiming **intentional infliction of emotional distress (IIED)**. Like defamation, IIED is governed by the common law and varies state by state. It most commonly requires the speaker to make an "outrageous" statement that "exceeds all bounds of decency tolerated in a civilized society," with the intent to cause emotional harm to another person. Should this kind of speech be afforded more or less protection than defamation under the First Amendment?

In 1983, *Hustler* magazine ran a parody ad that made fun of right-wing evangelical preacher Jerry Falwell. It spoofed a then-popular series of Campari ads in which celebrities gave testimonials, laced with double entendres, that described their "first time," revealing at the end that they were talking only about drinking Campari. *Hustler* published a mock interview with Falwell in which he described *his* "first time" as getting drunk on Campari and then having sex with his mother in an outhouse. The ad also implied that he routinely preached while drunk, including the fake quote: "I always get sloshed before I go out to the pulpit. You don't think I could lay down all that bullshit *sober*, do you?" Falwell sued the magazine and won a $150,000 judgement for IIED. The Supreme Court took up the appeal to decide whether the Sullivan Test should apply in IIED, as well as defamation, cases.

The justices in *Hustler Magazine v. Falwell* (1988) ruled 8–0 that the Sullivan Test did apply and overturned the damage award. A large part of the majority opinion was devoted to the history of protection that U.S. law had given to parody and satire. While *Hustler's* ad fell outside the normal standards of political cartoons and satirical commentary, the Court held that juries do not have the right to decide what kinds of commentary are so "outrageous" as to be outside the bounds of First Amendment protection.

If you think this statement directly contradicts the "contemporary community standards" prong of the Miller Test, you're absolutely right! But, that's how it goes sometimes with the Supreme Court. The takeaway from *Falwell* is that it's almost impossible for a public figure to recover damages for IIED if the offensive statement was made as a parody, satire, or commentary. Perhaps if *Hustler* made factual, non-joking claims that Jerry Falwell had actually engaged in an incestuous relationship with his mother they would have lost, but that's about how blatant it would need to have been.

Ok, so if the Supreme Court has extended First Amendment protection to speech concerning public figures in IIED cases, does this also mean that speech concerning private figures should be against IIED suits? The case of *Snyder v. Phelps* (2011) brought this question to the fore in the most graphic way imaginable.

The Westboro Baptist Church (WBC) was a religious congregation whose major activity is traveling around the country and picketing public events with signs displaying highly offensive messages. Led by the late Pastor Fred Phelps, the church advanced a message that God punishes the United States for tolerating homosexuality, abortion, Jews, Catholics, Muslims, and a litany of other purported sins and sinners.

Lance Corporal Matthew A. Snyder was killed in action in Iraq in 2006, and his funeral was scheduled to take place at a Catholic church in his hometown of Westminster, MD. When Fred Phelps learned of the funeral and the fact that Matthew Snyder's father, Albert Snyder, was gay, the WBC decided to picket the funeral. The WBC informed the town that it was planning a protest and had complied with all local ordinances. Members assembled on public land approximately 1,000 feet from the church entrance, holding signs that read: "God Hates the U.S.A.," "Thank God for 9/11," "Thank God for Dead Soldiers," "Thank God for IEDs," "Pope in Hell," "Priests Rape Boys," "God Hates Fags," "You're Going to Hell," and "God Hates You." Albert Snyder sued Phelps and the WBC for IIED and won a $5 million damage award, which was appealed to the Supreme Court.

An 8–1 majority overturned the damage award and ruled in favor of Phelps and the WBC, finding that their speech was protected by the First Amendment even though it concerned a private figure only. The fact that the WBC picketers were located on a "traditional public forum" also seemed to sway some members of the Court; Chief Justice John Roberts wrote: "Simply put, the church members had the right to be where they were." Justice Alito was unconvinced and wrote a vigorous solo dissent, arguing that the WBC's signs were directed against the Snyders personally and that extending the First Amendment to block IIED claims by private figures would only "allow the brutalization of innocent victims like [Corporal Snyder]."

As a brief aside, *Snyder* marked the first time that the Supreme Court used the TPM language of a "traditional public forum" in a defamation/IIED decision. The Court previously had used the term to designate areas where the *government* could not impose content-based restrictions on speech without satisfying strict scrutiny. In *Snyder* it extended such protection to the realm of private lawsuits. Was the fact that the WBC picketers were in a traditional public forum a major part of the decision, or just additional "juice" to support the majority's argument? The justices didn't really say. Alito did point out in his dissent that the Court had never held either fighting words or defamatory speech to be protected just because they took place in a traditional public forum. Does this mean that a majority of justices will apply TPM classifications in defamation and IIED cases? After *Snyder*, this is an open question.

# ✦ 15 ✦

## CORPORATIONS ARE PEOPLE, MY FRIEND: IS MONEY THE SAME THING AS SPEECH?

**T**HIS IS THE CHAPTER—PERHAPS THE ONE YOU'VE been waiting for—in which we explore the recent controversy over the question of whether money equals speech. We tackle this question by looking at two different types of cases: the first dealing with government attempts to regulate commercial speech, the second concerning the regulation of money in political campaigns.

Let's start with commercial speech. This might come as a surprise to you, but before 1976, commercial speech had no First Amendment protection whatsoever. In the case of *Valentine v. Chrestensen* (1942), decided the same year as *Chaplinksy,* the Supreme Court issued a short opinion that declared:

> *The Constitution imposes no . . . restraint on government as respects purely commercial advertising.*

Simply put, issues of commercial speech "are matters for legislative judgment." The Supreme Court was announcing that it would not overrule any laws that restrict commercial speech, grouping them with fighting words, obscenity, and defamation as a categorical exclusion to the First Amendment.

Things began to change in the early 1970s. In *Virginia State Pharmacy Board v. Virginia Citizens Consumer Council* (1976), a majority of the Supreme Court took the issue head on. Justice Blackmun, writing for the majority, overruled *Valentine* and struck down a Virginia law forbidding pharmacists from advertising drug prices: "Our question, then, is whether [commercial] communication is wholly outside the protection of the First Amendment. . . . Our answer is that it is not." In a statement that would echo in future cases, the Court asserted:

*It is clear . . . that speech does not lose its First Amendment protection because money is spent to project it.*

This still left the door open for the government to regulate commercial speech based on TPM restrictions, "false and misleading" advertising, or goods that are already illegal. Justice Rehnquist issued the sole dissent to the ruling at hand and, in oracular fashion, expressed fear that the majority's decision would open the way for the direct advertising of drugs on radio and television.

While the decision in *Virginia State Pharmacy Board* extended First Amendment protection to commercial speech, it did not determine what standard of review the Court would apply. Would it be strict scrutiny, as in most other content-based restrictions on speech, or a deferential standard that gives the government more leeway?

The Court finally settled on an approach in *Central Hudson Gas & Electric Corp. v. Public Service Commission* (1980). An 8–1 majority (with Rehnquist again the sole dissenter) voted to strike down a New York regulation that banned utility companies from running ads designed to promote electricity usage. The Court settled on an intermediate scrutiny standard for commercial speech, with Justice Powell's laying out a concise, four-part test:

1. Does the commercial speech concern a lawful, non-misleading activity?

2. Does the government have a substantial interest in regulating the activity?

3. If the answers to questions 1 and 2 are both yes, does the regulation directly advance the government's asserted interest?

4. If the answer to question 3 is yes, is the regulation no more extensive than necessary to further that interest?

Going through the facts of the case, the majority concluded that while New York's interest in conserving energy was substantial and that the regulation directly advanced its interest, the complete advertising ban was more extensive than necessary, rendering it unconstitutional.

Justice Rehnquist won a little vindication six years later in the case of *Posadas de Puerto Rico Associates v. Tourism Company of Puerto Rico* (1986). The core question here was whether commercial speech promoting harmful but not illegal activities such as alcohol consumption, tobacco use, and gambling should be protected by the First Amendment.

Puerto Rico had legalized casino gambling in the 1940s to bring in tourist dollars, but banned casino advertising on the island to limit participation by residents. The owners of several casinos sued to overturn the law. Justice Rehnquist, writing the 5–4 opinion of the Court, determined that Puerto Rico's advertising ban was constitutional even though gambling was legal. The desire to protect the "health, safety, and welfare" of residents by keeping them away from casino gambling qualified as a substantial government interest, the Court ruled. Moreover, the law directly advanced that interest, and it was not more extensive than necessary because it still allowed casinos to advertise on the U.S. mainland. Finally, because a complete ban on casino gambling was within the authority of the government, it could also "take the less intrusive step of allowing the conduct, but reducing the demand through restrictions on advertising." The dissenting justices argued that attempts to "deprive consumers of accurate information concerning lawful activity" should have to pass strict scrutiny and that the law discriminated between speakers based on their intended audience.

183

After *Posadas*, it appeared that the Court might be carving out an exception for the regulation of "vice" activities. A decade later, however, the justices shot down any broad notion of a vice exception in *Rubin v. Coors Brewing Co.* (1995), unanimously overturning a federal ban on listing alcohol content on beer labels. Justice Thomas left no doubt about the majority's opinion when he wrote: "Legislatures [do not] have broader latitude to regulate speech that promotes socially harmful activities, such as alcohol consumption, than they have to regulate other types of speech." One year later, the Court would deal another blow to *Posadas* in *44 Liquormart, Inc. v. Rhode Island* (1996).

The *44 Liquormart* case dealt with a challenge by a discount liquor retailer to a Rhode Island law that prohibited the advertisement of the price of alcoholic beverages "in any manner whatsoever." A unanimous Supreme Court voted to strike down law, with *Posadas* again coming in for harsh treatment. A four-justice plurality led by Justice Stevens argued that the case should be explicitly overruled. The majority opinion in *Posadas* "cannot be reconciled" with the Court's other commercial speech cases, they maintained, and was "inconsistent with both logic and well-settled doctrine." Finally, to avoid any confusion

whatsoever, the plurality rejected the notion of a vice exception in explicit terms: "the scope of any [vice] exception to the protection afforded by the First Amendment would be difficult, if not impossible, to define." Although Justice Stevens couldn't get a fifth vote to overturn *Posadas,* the Court's rulings in *Rubin* and *44 Liquormart* left that decision in a state of limbo. *Posadas* is now a legal zombie—still shuffling around but with very little vitality—while *Central Hudson Gas* remains the seminal test in commercial speech cases.

With all that said about money-as-speech in commercial advertising, we shift now to the political arena. The Supreme Court has stated on numerous occasions that political speech forms the core of the First Amendment's freedoms and is entitled to the highest degree of protection. Under no circumstances can the government regulate an individual's ability to speak his or her mind on candidates or issues of the day. But does this include spending money on political campaigns? Is money spent on political advocacy really just speech in another form? Or should money be treated more like symbolic speech in *O'Brien* (the draft card-burning case in Chapter 9) since spending is a form of conduct?

Note that important public policy issues are at play here. Unlike traditional speech, which any citizen can engage in equally, some citizens necessarily have more money than others to spend on political campaigns. Is it fair to allow a rich person who can afford to spend millions of dollars on a campaign to speak with a voice millions of times greater than people who don't have the same resources? Or does the First Amendment trump those concerns (pardon the pun once again)? Money in politics also creates the appearance of corruption and quid pro quo expectations. It's hard to imagine a donor cutting a seven-figure check to a candidate and expecting little more than a handshake in return. This is why money-as-speech is such an explosive issue. It cuts to the very heart of our democratic system, pitting free speech and property rights against political equality and good government.

President Theodore Roosevelt championed campaign finance reform in the early 20th century, and Congress followed up by passing a series of laws regulating the amount of money corporations and trade unions could donate to candidates for federal office. In 1971, these

Well, y'know, there ought to be a LIMIT to what unions and corporations can raise for campaign funds.

Theodore Roosevelt

laws were combined and streamlined along with several others as part of the Federal Election Campaign Act (FECA). The FECA underwent massive changes in 1974, in the fallout after the Watergate scandal. The new amendments were the most comprehensive attempt to overhaul federal elections that Congress had ever undertaken. They capped individual political contributions at $1,000 per candidate per election cycle; limited private expenditures on behalf of a candidate at $1,000 per year; limited total political contributions at $25,000 per year; and limited the amount of their own money candidates could spend on their campaigns. The new regulations were challenged as soon as they were signed into law by President Gerald Ford and came before the Supreme Court in the landmark case of *Buckley v. Valeo* (1976).

*Buckley* can be a difficult decision to understand both because the law is complex and because the Court fractured into six different opinions, with various justices concurring in some parts and dissenting in others. Let's sort things out by looking at the major points one at a time. First, a majority rejected the argument that spending money on political campaigns should be reviewed as symbolic speech under the O'Brien Test: "The expenditure of money simply cannot be equated with such conduct as the destruction of a draft card." Because "virtually every means of communicating ideas in today's mass society requires the expenditure of money," the Court decided to treat campaign spending as the equivalent of traditional speech. The majority held that the government may regulate money in politics only if it has a "sufficiently important interest" and if the means employed to advance that interest are "closely drawn to avoid unnecessary abridgement of [speech]."

Under this test, the majority concluded that the contribution limits pass muster. Since the legislation's "primary purpose—to limit the actuality and appearance of corruption resulting from large individual financial contributions" was "constitutionally sufficient justification" for the contribution limits, the Court concluded that such limits were narrowly tailored enough to advance the government's interest. This is an important point to keep in mind. The Court recognized here that the government's interest in limiting even the *appearance* of impropriety or quid pro quo relationship between donors and office holders is important enough to justify some abridgement of free speech rights.

The spending limits came in for different treatment. The majority found these to "impose significantly more severe restrictions on protected freedoms of political expression" than the contribution limits and that they directly "limit political expression." The majority also rejected the government's interest in equalizing the ability of citizens to influence elections regardless of personal wealth as "not sufficient to justify the provision's infringement of fundamental First Amendment rights" and "wholly at odds with the guarantees of the First Amendment."

Justice Byron White wrote a powerfully worded dissent in which he flat-out rejected the proposition that money equals speech, since "money is not always equivalent to or used for speech, even in political campaigns." He also argued that the majority gave insufficient weight to significant government interests—that is, to "restore and maintain public confidence in federal elections . . . [and] to obviate or dispel the impression that federal elections are purely and simply a function of money." Both Justice White and Justice Marshall agreed that Congress also has a significant interest in "equaliz[ing] access to the political arena" and "encouraging the less wealthy . . . to run for political office."

The decision in *Buckley* made it clear that expenditure limits almost always violate the First Amendment. But it did not touch on the question of whether the First Amendment protects political spending by corporations as well as by individuals. A case raising this issue landed on the desks of the justices only two years later in *First National Bank of Boston v. Bellotti* (1978).

As part of the wave of post-Watergate electoral reforms sweeping the country in the mid-1970s, the Massachusetts legislature passed a law restricting the ability of corporations to spend money on political advertising for ballot initiatives not "materially affecting any of the property, business or assets of the corporation." A number of Boston banks and financial institutions sued to overturn the law when they were prohibited from running ads opposing a ballot measure on the state income tax. The Supreme Court voted 5–4 to overturn the Massachusetts statute for violating the First Amendment. Justice Powell, writing for the majority, mostly avoided the question of whether corporations have constitutional rights. The question was "not whether corporations 'have' First Amendment rights, and, if so, whether they are coextensive with those of natural persons," he wrote, but whether the law "abridges expression that the First Amendment was meant to protect." Elsewhere he took a stronger approach by overruling prior cases and rejecting "the proposition that speech that otherwise would be within the protection of the First Amendment loses that protection simply because its source is a corporation."

Justice White, in a dissent joined by Justices Marshall and Brennan, maintained that corporations, unlike natural persons, can speak only through other people (most likely its board of directors). To recognize

corporate free speech rights would compel some shareholders to "support and financially further beliefs with which they disagree." Moreover, White wrote, the government has a heightened interest in regulating corporate speech since its special status allows it "to control vast amounts of economic power which may, if not regulated, dominate not only the economy but also the very heart of our democracy, the electoral process." Since corporations are endowed with these special privileges by the state, "the State need not permit its own creation to consume it." Justice Rehnquist expanded on this argument in a separate dissent, noting that since corporations are created by state-granted charters, the states are free to endow them with whatever rights they wish.

*Bellotti* seemed to remove any doubt that corporate political speech was protected by the First Amendment. Case closed—or so it seemed. Out of nowhere, however, the dissenters in *Buckley* and *Bellotti* struck back in the 1990 case of *Austin v. Michigan Chamber of Commerce.* This was in many ways a parting shot from the corporate-speech skeptics on the Court. Justice Brennan would retire at the end of the term, Justice Marshall retired the following year, and both Justice White and Justice Blackmun would retire in three years. One has to wonder if they didn't realize that this would be their last opportunity to limit corporate spending in political campaigns.

Michigan had passed a law restricting corporations from spending money from their general treasuries on political campaigns but allowing them to spend money from specially segregated political funds set up for that purpose. For the first time since *Buckley,* the Court decided, 6–3, to uphold the campaign finance restriction. Justice Marshall's majority opinion reads like *Bellotti* in reverse. Because of the "unique legal and economic characteristics of corporations," he argued, the government has an important interest in regulating their speech so they don't "use 'resources amassed in the economic marketplace' to obtain 'an unfair advantage in the political marketplace.'" As a balance against the "corrosive and distorting effects of immense aggregations of wealth that are accumulated with the help of the corporate form," the majority concluded that a state might limit corporate political spending only to separate funds set aside for this purpose. Justice Scalia, writing in dissent, decried the majority opinion as an "Orwellian announcement" that replaced free speech rights with a government-knows-best approach when it comes to ensuring "the 'fairness' of political debate." Justices Kennedy and O'Connor, also dissenting, viewed the majority opinion as incompatible with *Buckley* and *Bellotti.* In any event, *Austin* would prove to be an outlier and the last gasp of any attempt to limit money in politics.

One of the most popular methods that campaign finance lawyers had devised to skirt contribution limits was by giving so-called "soft money" donations to political parties. As long as the funds were not directed to an individual candidate, they were not considered a "contribution" under the FECA—thereby allowing unlimited donations to the parties. In an attempt to ban soft money, Senators John McCain and Russ Feingold joined with Chris Shays and Marty Meehan in the House to sponsor the most comprehensive campaign finance regulation since the FECA: the Bipartisan Campaign Reform Act of 2002, commonly known as McCain-Feingold.

Opponents of McCain-Feingold acted as soon as the law went into effect. Leading the charge was Senator Mitch McConnell, who had tried on several occasions to block passage of the bill through filibusters in the Senate. McConnell sued the Federal Election Committee (FEC) to block enforcement

of the law, and the Supreme Court took up the case in *McConnell v. FEC* (2003). The justices wrote eight different opinions, touching on twenty-one different sections of the law, to create a 300-page monster of a decision. The important takeaway is that they upheld most of McCain-Feingold, including the ban on soft money. A majority also reaffirmed the principle that the government has a significant interest in preventing "both the actual corruption threatened by large financial contributions and the eroding of public confidence in the electoral process through the appearance of corruption."

Defeat in the Supreme Court did nothing to deter the opponents of campaign finance reform from keeping up the pressure. Changes in the Court's membership had also made the overall balance of the justices much more corporate-friendly. Even though *Buckley* made it clear that contribution limits did not violate the First Amendment, a 6–3 majority in *Randall v. Sorell* (2006) overturned Vermont's contribution limits for being unconstitutionally low. The high court chipped away a piece of McCain-Feingold the following year in *FEC v. Wisconsin Right to Life, Inc.* (2007), when it invalidated the portion of the act prohibiting corporations from running issue ads thirty days before a primary or sixty days before a general election. The language of the decision was telling. Chief Justice John Roberts had little patience for the government's arguments, declaring: "Enough is enough. . . . [W]e give the benefit of the doubt to speech, not censorship. The First Amendment's command that 'Congress shall make no law . . . abridging the freedom of speech' demands at least that." Justices Scalia, Kennedy, and Thomas would have overruled both *Austin* and *McConnell* outright.

The following year, in *Davis v. FEC* (2008), the Court struck down the so-called "Millionaire's Amendment" to McCain-Feingold, which had limited the amount of contributions candidates could accept if they spent more than $350,000 of their own money on their campaign. Justice Alito, writing for the majority, explained that since *Buckley* recognized no legitimate government interest "in equalizing the financial resources of candidates," it could not apply different contribution limits to different candidates based on their personal finances. Justice Stevens argued vigorously in dissent that the Court had gone wildly off-track since *Buckley v. Valeo*, constitutionalizing a money-charged political climate that turned debate into "a shouting match that awards points on the basis of decibels rather than reasons." He argued that the limitation on money in politics has nothing to do with the content of speech and should therefore be analyzed as a TPM restriction.

Justice Stevens's arguments rang hollow as a 5–4 majority dropped the hammer on campaign finance reform two years later in the landmark case of *Citizens United v. FEC* (2010). The core issue in *Citizens United* combined those of *Austin* and *McConnell:* Can the government prohibit corporations from spending general treasury funds on "electioneering communications" thirty days before a primary or sixty days before a general election?

The group Citizens United, a conservative nonprofit corporation, had filed a complaint with the FEC in 2004 alleging that Michael Moore's film *Fahrenheit 911* constituted illegal electioneering communications in violation of McCain-Feingold. The FEC dismissed the complaint on the grounds that the film was a "bona fide commercial activity" rather than an electioneering communication. In response, Citizens United decided to directly challenge the law by running political advertising under the guise of a documentary. The organization created a feature-length production called *Hillary: The Movie*, attacking Democratic presidential candidate Hillary Clinton, and planned to run commercials advertising the film within thirty days of the 2008 Democratic primary in several states. Citizens United then initiated a federal lawsuit to prohibit the FEC from blocking it from running the ads. After the District Court ruled in favor of the FEC, Citizens United appealed to the Supreme Court.

By a 5–4 vote, the Court struck down the core provision of the McCain-Feingold Act as an unconstitutional restriction on the right of corporate speech. The majority opinion, written by Justice Kennedy, made clear the direction it would take by beginning its analysis with a statement of precedent—"The Court has recognized that First Amendment protection extends to corporations"—and then took a hatchet to both *Austin* and *McConnell.* The former, Kennedy declared, "was not well reasoned" and "abandoned First Amendment principles." Just so there was no confusion, he then delivered *Austin*'s eulogy:

*Due consideration leads to this conclusion: Austin should be and now is overruled. We return to the principle established in Buckley and Bellotti that the government may not suppress political speech on the basis of the speaker's corporate identity.*

From this point on, the only significant government interest the Supreme Court would recognize for limiting money in politics was preventing actual quid pro quo corruption. A desire to remove the appearance of impropriety or get money out of the political arena would no longer be good enough. The portion of *McConnell* that recognized the government's ability to place greater speech restrictions on corporations than on private individuals also fell by the wayside, with the majority holding that "political speech does not lose First Amendment protection 'simply because its source is a corporation.'"

Without the support of either *Austin* or *McConnell*, McCain-Feingold didn't stand a chance. Kennedy's majority opinion found the provision to be "an outright ban, backed by criminal sanctions. . . . If the First Amendment has any force, it prohibits Congress from fining or jailing citizens, or associations of citizens, for simply engaging in political speech." Henceforth, corporations would have the same First Amendment rights as people to engage in political speech, and neither the federal government nor the states could restrict money in politics for anything short of preventing quid pro quo corruption.

Justice Stevens had recently announced his retirement at the end of the term and left it all on the table in a scathing dissent. Joined by Justices Ginsburg, Breyer, and Sotomayor, Justice Stevens blasted the majority opinion for threatening "to undermine the integrity of elected institutions across the Nation" and lamented that "[t]he path it has taken to reach its outcome will, I fear, do damage to this institution." The idea that corporations have the same constitutional rights as natural persons is "a dramatic break from our past," he wrote. Having "no consciences, no beliefs, no feelings, no thoughts, no desires" of their own, corporations "are not themselves members of 'We the People' by whom and for whom the Constitution was established."

Stevens also dismissed as "facile" the majority's argument "that there is no such thing as too much speech," since "corporate domination of the airwaves" has a tendency to drown out all other forms of speech and "generate the impression that corporations dominate our democracy. . . . The predictable result is cynicism and disenchantment." Similarly, he argued against limiting the legitimate government interest in preventing quid pro quo corruption, since the appearance of "undue influence" by corporations is "far more destructive to a democratic society than the odd bribe. . . . In a functioning democracy the public must have faith that its representatives owe their positions to the people, not to the corporations with the deepest pockets." And so, Justice Stevens wrote with uncommon passion,

*The Court's blinkered and aphoristic approach to the First Amendment may well promote corporate power at the cost of the individual and collective self-expression the [First] Amendment was meant to serve. It will undoubtedly cripple the ability of ordinary citizens, Congress, and the States to adopt even limited measures to protect against corporate domination of the electoral process. Americans may be forgiven if they do not feel the Court has advanced the cause of self-government today.*

In the years following *Citizens United,* the Supreme Court has continued to use the First Amendment to strike down attempts at campaign finance reform. In the 2011 case of *Arizona Free Enterprise Club's Freedom Club PAC v. Bennett,* a 5–4 majority voted to strike down an Arizona law that provided public money to candidates who were outspent by their opponents, arguing that a desire to "level the playing field" is not a significant enough interest to justify the burden on political speech. Three years later, in *McCutcheon v. FEC* (2014), the same five justices whittled down contribution limits even further, holding that the government cannot impose a limit on how much money a person can contribute in one year.

After all that, the only major parts of McCain-Feingold left standing were the individual contribution limits to a single federal candidate ($2,700 per election cycle in 2017–18) and the soft money restrictions. The government is barred by the First Amendment from doing nearly anything to prohibit unlimited political spending by either individuals or corporations.

# ✦ 16 ✦

## CAN THE FOURTH ESTATE BE (PRIORLY) RESTRAINED?

"FREE SPEECH"

"SUBVERSIVE PROPAGANDA"

I N ADDITION TO ITS BROAD PROTECTIONS FOR FREEDOM
of speech, the First Amendment also guarantees freedom of the
press. But what exactly *is* "the press?" Does the First Amendment
grant some special status to a private enterprise, and if so, should
that cover only institutional media like newspapers and magazines, or
should it include all publications, including blogs and social media
posts? And how far does this freedom extend? Does the First Amendment's Press Clause guarantee rights beyond those already covered
under freedom of speech—such as prohibiting the government from
blocking or punishing journalists who publish leaked information?

You may find this hard to believe, but the Supreme Court has never definitively answered the question of who or what qualifies as "the press." The strongest proponent of the press-as-institutional-media was Justice Potter Stewart. According to Justice Stewart, the Press Clause "extends protection to an institution," and the media are the "only organized private business given explicit constitutional protection." This is because the institutional media play an important role as the Fourth Estate, acting as "an additional check on the three official branches."

The majority of the Supreme Court has not embraced this approach, however. Chief Justice Warren Burger expressed some of the strongest anti-press-as-institutional-media language when he declared: "I can see no difference between the right of those who seek to disseminate ideas by way of a newspaper and those who give lectures or speeches. . . . [T]he First Amendment does not 'belong' to any identifiable category of persons or entities: it belongs to all who exercise its freedoms." Perhaps because of the difficulty in determining who or what qualifies as the press, the justices have tended to shy away from recognizing special constitutional protections for the institutional media. Except when they don't.

One form of government action that has long been disfavored in U.S. law is called **prior restraint**. This is a form of censorship in which the government uses its power to prevent a person or institution from speaking, typically through a court-issued injunction or the kind of restrictive press licensing systems that existed in the colonies prior to independence (see Chapter 2). The U.S. Supreme Court hinted that the First Amendment might prohibit states from enacting prior restraint on news organizations in *Patterson v. Colorado* (1907), but it did not definitively rule on the issue until its first major freedom of the press decision in *Near v. Minnesota* (1931).

Minnesota had passed the most restrictive press "gag law" in the nation in 1925, allowing courts to issue permanent injunctions against anyone publishing a "malicious, scandalous and defamatory news-paper, or other periodical." The *Saturday Press*, a Minneapolis paper run by two controversial editors, ran a headline story claiming that "a Jew-ish gangster was in control of gambling, bootlegging and racketeering in Minneapolis" and accusing the chief of police of joining in "illicit relations with gangsters [and] participation in graft." A local prose-cutor filed for an injunction based on the gag law, and the trial court issued an order permanently barring the editors from ever publishing the *Saturday Press* or any other publication containing similar material. The U.S. Supreme Court took up the appeal after the Minnesota Supreme Court found the law to be constitutional.

A five-justice majority disagreed with the Minnesota Supreme Court and struck down the law for violating the Press Clause of the First Amendment. According to the majority, a "chief purpose" of the First Amendment is to "prevent previous restraints upon publi-cation." Justice Hughes, writing for the majority, quoted extensively from Blackstone and described the long fight against press censor-ship in England. The First Amendment was designed to eliminate this practice, he wrote, and Minnesota's gag law was "the essence of censorship."

This was the first time that the U.S. Supreme Court specifically mentioned the "liberty of the press" and the "immunity of the press from previous constraint" in overturning a law. But the ruling included a caveat: First Amendment protections "even as to previous restraint are not absolutely unlimited" and may be justified "in exceptional cases," such as "actual obstruction" of wartime efforts or "incitements to acts of violence and the overthrow by force of orderly government." Since none of these were present in *Near*, the question of when the "national security exception" to prior restraint kicks in was left for a later court to decide.

Fast-forward forty years, and the country is in crisis. In spite of President Nixon's pledge to end the Vietnam War after his election in 1968, there is still no end in sight three years later. Nixon is facing reelection and desperately wants to show a war-weary nation that he is making progress toward the goal of "peace with honor." But his hopes are dashed in June 1971, when he learns that Daniel Ellsberg, a former Pentagon official, has leaked classified information to the *New York Times* and *Washington Post* detailing the full scope of U.S. involvement in Southeast Asia. The revelations prove damning. The information contained in the "Pentagon Papers," as they came to be called, show nearly three decades of covert activity, lies, political assassinations, and deceit by the Truman, Eisenhower, Kennedy, and Johnson administrations. Nixon springs into action, ordering his attorney general to use the Espionage Act of 1917 to bring criminal charges against Ellsberg and file for an injunction blocking the *Times* and *Post* from publishing the classified documents. The courts split, with one granting an injunction against the *Times* and another denying an injunction against the *Post*. Given the sensitivity and importance of the issues at hand, the Supreme Court took up both appeals days later in *New York Times Co. v. United States* (1971), also known as the Pentagon Papers Case.

Because of the time crunch, the ruling came in at a whopping three paragraphs, declaring:

> *Any system of prior restraints of expression comes to this Court bearing a heavy presumption against its constitutional validity. The Government thus carries a heavy burden of showing justification for the enforcement of such a restraint. . . . [T]he Government has not met that burden.*

Each of the justices wrote a separate opinion, six in favor of overturning the injunction and three opposed. Although the opinions are disjointed, most boil down to one central question: How should the Court weigh the constitutional freedom of the press, particularly in the case of a prior restraint, against the constitutional authority of the president in matters of national security?

Justices Black and Douglas, the two First Amendment absolutists on the high court, came down most strongly in favor of press freedom. To Justice Black, the press enjoys special constitutional protection "so that it could bare the secrets of government and inform the people. Only a free and unrestrained press can effectively expose deception in government." Allowing any prior restraint based on the president's "inherent power," Black argued, would "make a shambles of the First Amendment." He also dismissed the concept of a "national security" justification for restricting press freedom as "a broad, vague generality whose contours should not be invoked to abrogate the fundamental law embodied in the First Amendment." Justice Douglas joined in by pointing out that the limited exceptions in *Near* applied only in wartime and that Congress had never issued a declaration of war in Vietnam.

Justice Brennan agreed that the *Near* exceptions applied only during a declared war and that the government had given the Court no good reason to expand that holding. Perhaps if a prior restraint was needed to prevent "a nuclear holocaust" the Court would allow it, Brennan wrote, but no such evidence was presented here. The government's argument that the leaked information "'could,' or 'might,' or 'may' prejudice the national interest" was insufficient to block publication, he held, since "the First Amendment tolerates absolutely no prior judicial restraints of the press predicated upon surmise or conjecture." Since neither the *New York Times* nor *Washington Post* was breaking the law by publishing the information, according to Justice Marshal, the Nixon Administration was attempting to "invoke the contempt power of a court" to do what it otherwise could not.

Justices Stewart and White also concurred, but in a much less full-throated way. Both of their opinions have a somewhat pained tone and read almost like dissents. Stewart argues at length that "[t]he Executive must have the largely unshared duty" to protect national security "as a matter of sovereign prerogative and not as a matter of law as the courts know law." In his view, the "only effective restraint upon executive policy and power in the areas of national defense and international affairs [is] an enlightened citizenry." Justice White also joined with the majority, "but only because of the concededly extraordinary protection against prior restraints enjoyed by the press under our constitutional system."

The three dissenters were furious. Each of them slammed the majority for rushing out a decision on such a sensitive issue. Justice Harlan described the process as "irresponsibly feverish," on a timetable that was "wholly inadequate for giving these cases the kind of consideration they deserve." Chief Justice Burger characterized the proceedings as having been "conducted in unseemly haste" and admitted, "we literally do not know what we are acting on."

To be sure, the dissenters also took issue with the substance of the decision. Justice Harlan's bone of contention was the questioning of presidential judgment about national security matters that are "political, not judicial." He also insinuated that the majority's easy dismissal of the administration's national security rationale was based on the justices' own views of President Nixon and the conduct of the Vietnam War: "I can see no indication . . . that the conclusions of the Executive were given even the deference owing to an administrative agency, must less that owing to a co-equal branch of the Government."

Justice Blackmun lamented the lack of an objective test by which the justices could weigh, "upon properly developed standards," the "broad right of the press to print" against "the very narrow right of the Government to prevent." Since the Court had not created such a test and was "in disagreement as to what those standards should be," Justice Blackmun would have kept the injunction in place as the case made its way through the lower courts. He also believed that the release of the Pentagon documents could result in great harm to the nation, including "the death of soldiers," "destruction of alliances," "greatly increased difficulty of negotiation with our enemies," "prolongation of the war," and "further delay in the freeing of [POWs]."

Let's shift direction a bit here and explore a hypothetical situation . . . . What if, instead of seeking prior restraint, President Nixon had gotten Congress to impose punitive taxes on the newspapers? There is no constitutional requirement that taxes must be distributed evenly across all sectors of the population. The Supreme Court has allowed the states nearly unlimited power to structure their tax systems however they see fit and has interpreted Congress's income tax power under the Sixteenth Amendment very broadly. So can the government use the power to tax as a stick to beat a recalcitrant press into submission?

The Supreme Court has blocked some taxes that violate other provisions of the Constitution. In the early landmark case of *McCullough v. Maryland* (1819), Chief Justice Marshall struck down a Maryland tax on the Bank of the United States, famously declaring: "The power to tax involves the power to destroy." During the Civil Rights era, in *Harper v. Virginia Board of Elections* (1966), the high court struck down poll taxes as a violation of the Fourteenth Amendment's Equal Protection Clause. The first time the Supreme Court struck down a tax on a private entity, however, was in a Press Clause case.

*Grosjean v. American Press Co.* (1936) arose out of the politically charged atmosphere of Louisiana under Governor Huey Long. The Kingfish, as he was known, had established himself as America's premier populist, capturing the Louisiana governorship in 1928 on a campaign motto of "Every Man a King." When the largest newspapers in the state began to run negative headlines about him, Long had his allies in the state legislature pass a two percent "tax on lying" that applied only to them. The newspapers immediately challenged the levy on the grounds that it violated the First Amendment. While the case was making its way through the courts, Long's political career came to an abrupt end by an assassin's bullet in September 1935, one month after he had declared his candidacy for president.

Long's death won his "liar's tax" no sympathy with the Supreme Court. In a unanimous decision, the justices struck down the tax as an unconstitutional infringement on the freedom of the press. The opinion, by Justice George Sutherland, embraced the "Fourth Estate" justification of the Press Clause, finding that the Constitution specifically protects the press "as one of the great interpreters between the government and the people. To allow it to be fettered is to fetter ourselves." The tax in this instance was deemed "bad not because it takes money from the pockets of the [newspapers] . . . [but because] it is seen to be a deliberate and calculated device in the guise of a tax to limit the circulation of information to which the public is entitled to in virtue of the constitutional guaranties."

The Supreme Court would not rule again on press taxation until *Minneapolis Star & Tribune v. Minnesota Commissioner of Revenue* (1983). This case presented a far more mundane but no less important issue. Minnesota had implemented a "use tax" on anybody using more than $100,000 of paper and ink in a calendar year. The burden fell overwhelmingly on the largest newspaper publishers in the state, such as the *Minneapolis Star & Tribune*, which alone paid nearly two-thirds of the tax receipts. Even though there was no evidence of discriminatory intent, as in *Grosjean*, the Court struck down the tax for violating the Press Clause. As Justice O'Connor, writing for the eight-justice majority, explained:

> *Differential taxation of the press, then, places such a burden on the interests protected by the First Amendment that we cannot countenance such treatment unless the State asserts a counterbalancing interest of compelling importance that it cannot achieve without differential taxation.*

In a nutshell, if a state wants to impose a special tax on the press, the measure needs to satisfy strict scrutiny. While this sounds like a First Amendment shield protecting the institutional media against certain kinds of taxes, we can't be certain how far it extends since the Supreme Court has not revisited the issue again since 1983. It would be interesting now to see if the same shield would apply to bloggers, podcasters, and others outside the institutional media.

The final Press Clause issue we will address is whether the government can compel journalists to reveal their sources or disclose information they obtained during the course of an investigation. As a general rule, anybody can be compelled to testify in a legal proceeding by being served with a subpoena. A person who refuses to testify will be held in contempt of court and subject to fines or imprisonment. In some cases, however, a person can refuse to testify on the basis of a privilege. The most common of these are attorney-client privilege, doctor-patient privilege, clerical privilege, and sometimes spousal privilege. Does the Press Clause of the First Amendment also establish a constitutional journalist's privilege in order to protect freedom of the press?

The Supreme Court ruled on this issue in *Branzburg v. Hayes* (1972). This case actually concerned three different journalists—one who had written a story on drug use in Kentucky and the other two who had written on the Black Panthers. All three had been subpoenaed to testify in front of grand juries during criminal investigations, and all three were convicted of contempt when they refused to identify their sources. The reporters appealed to the Supreme Court, claiming a First Amendment journalist's privilege. In a 5–4 decision, the Court rejected the claim that the First Amendment grants "newsmen a testimonial privilege that other citizens do not enjoy." The majority based its ruling on two main points. The first was that no court in the nation's history had ever recognized the existence of a constitutional journalist's privilege. The second was more pragmatic. Justice White's majority opinion reiterated the "traditional doctrine" of the Supreme Court that "liberty of the press is the right of the lonely pamphleteer as much as of the large metropolitan publisher." Moreover, White wrote, the "administration of a constitutional newsman's privilege would present practical and conceptual difficulties of a high order." How could courts determine who qualifies as a journalist? Would every amateur sleuth who self-publishes a monthly broadsheet be protected from revealing her sources? The majority was unwilling to draw such distinctions.

Justice Powell's concurrence gave the majority its needed fifth vote, but it also threw a large dose of ambiguity into the decision. Powell made clear that the majority did "not hold that newsmen, subpoenaed to testify before a grand jury, are without constitutional rights with respect to gathering of news or safeguarding their sources." Stressing that "no harassment of newsmen will be tolerated," Powell hinted that journalists may be able to assert privilege claims if they can show that the information they are being asked to give is not in "good faith, . . . bear[s] only a remote and tenuous relationship to the subject of the investigation, . . . or implicates confidential source relationships without a legitimate need of law enforcement." The trial court will then judge the claim based on its facts, "striking of a proper balance between freedom of the press and the obligation of all citizens to give relevant testimony with respect to criminal conduct." By taking a case-by-case approach, he argued, judges can weigh the "vital constitutional and societal interests" at play. Thus, while he sided with the majority in refusing to recognize a broad First Amendment journalist's privilege, Justice Powell assured journalists that "the courts will be available to newsmen under circumstances where legitimate First Amendment interests require protection."

Justices Stewart, Marshall, Brennan, and Douglas would have recognized a journalist's privilege in the First Amendment. While they took some solace that Powell's "enigmatic concurring opinion" meant that the Court might adopt a more "flexible view in the future," they feared that without constitutional protection, press freedoms would be jeopardized by the government's use of "unbridled subpoena power" and threaten "to annex the journalistic profession as an investigative arm." Therefore, Justices Stewart, Marshall, and Brennan would have allowed the government to compel a journalist to testify only if it could prove a "compelling and overriding" need for the information and demonstrate that the information could not be obtained "by alternative means less destructive of First Amendment rights." Justice Douglas, as a First Amendment absolutist, argued that not even such a limited exception could justify forcing a journalist "from appearing or testifying before a grand jury, unless the reporter himself is implicated in a crime. His immunity in my view is therefore quite complete."

The Supreme Court has never again taken up the issue of a journalist's privilege, but in the decades following *Branzburg*, Justice Powell's "enigmatic" opinion has won the day. Most state and federal judges weigh the interests of the government against those of the reporter on a case-by-case basis when deciding whether to compel a journalist to divulge confidential sources. In addition, three-quarters of the states have enacted some form of statutory immunity for reporters. And so, even if the First Amendment does not provide an absolute guarantee of privilege, journalists still have some protection against being compelled to give up their sources—an important right amid accusations of "fake news" and threats of prosecution from political leaders.

# FURTHER READING

Abrams, Floyd. *The Soul of the First Amendment.* New Haven, CT: Yale University Press, 2017.

Abrams, Floyd. *Speaking Freely: Trials of the First Amendment.* New York: Penguin Books, 2006.

Barron, Jerome A., and C. Thomas Dienes. *First Amendment Law in a Nutshell.* St. Paul, MN: Thomson/West, 2008.

Erwin Chemerinsky, and Howard Gillman. *Free Speech on Campus.* New Haven, CT: Yale University Press, 2017.

Finn, John E., The Great Courses. *The First Amendment and You: What Everyone Should Know.* [Audio Recording]. Chantilly, VA: Teaching Co., 2012.

Haynes, Charles C., Sam Chaltain, and Susan M. Glisson. *First Freedoms: A Documentary History of First Amendment Rights in America.* New York: Oxford University Press, 2006.

Healy, Thomas. *The Great Dissent: How Oliver Wendell Holmes Changed His Mind—and Changed the Course of Free Speech in America.* New York: Henry Holt, 2013.

Lewis, Anthony. *Freedom for the Thought That We Hate: A Biography of the First Amendment.* New York: Basic Books, 2007.

Lewis, Anthony: *Make No Law: The Sullivan Case and the First Amendment.* New York: Random House, 1991.

McWhirter, Robert J. *First Amendment: An Illustrated History.* Tempe, AZ: Constitution Press, 2017.

Neuborne, Burt. *Madison's Music: On Reading the First Amendment.* New York: The New Press, 2015.

Shiffrin, Steven H., Jesse H. Choper, and Frederick Schauer: *The First Amendment: Cases, Comments, Questions.* St. Paul, MN: West Academic Publishing, 2015.

Tedford, Thomas L., et al. *Freedom of Speech in the United States.* State College, PA: Strata Publishing, 2013.

Weaver, Russell. *Understanding the First Amendment,* 5th ed. New Providence, NJ: LexisNexis, 2014.

## Websites

Cornell Law School—Legal Information Institute, CRS Annotated Constitution, First Amendment: www.law.cornell.edu/anncon/html/amdt1toc_user.html

FindLaw—U.S. Constitution, First Amendment: http://constitution.findlaw.com/amendment1.html

First Amendment Center: www.firstamendmentcenter.org

First Amendment Library, Foundation for Individual Rights in Education (FIRE): www.thefire.org/first-amendment-library

National Constitution Center, Interactive Constitution—Amendment I: https://constitutioncenter.org/interactive-constitution/amendments/amendment-i

Oyez: www.oyez.org

United States Courts, First Amendment Activities: http://www.uscourts.gov/about-federal-courts/educational-resources/educational-activities/first-amendment-activities

# ABOUT THE AUTHOR

**MICHAEL LAMONICA** is a writer, lawyer, and historian whose previous works include *The French Revolutions For Beginners* (2014). After seven years of legal practice in the Connecticut Attorney General's Office and part-time university teaching, he returned to graduate studies in history, obtaining his MA at McGill University where he is currently working on his doctorate. His research focus is on the French Atlantic World, specifically the intersection of law, religion, and commerce in the colonization of North America and the Caribbean. Outside of work he enjoys tabletop gaming, pub trivia, skiing, and just about anything involving the water.

# ABOUT THE ILLUSTRATOR

**JEFF FALLOW** has been illustrating For Beginners books since 1999, when the series was published by Writers & Readers. Previous books include *Stanislavski For Beginners* by David Allen, *London For Beginners* by Nita Clarke, and his own titles *Scotland For Beginners* and *Wales For Beginners*. Jeff has worked as illustrator for Glasgow Museums and graphic designer for the National Health Service. He is Scottish and lives in the Kingdom of Fife, an ancient part of Scotland and the home of golf (which he doesn't play). His hobbies include taxidermy (using roadkill) and making steampunk creations (using overkill).

# THE FOR BEGINNERS® SERIES

www.forbeginnersbooks.com

# THE FOR BEGINNERS® SERIES

| | |
|---|---|
| THE HISTORY OF OPERA FOR BEGINNERS | ISBN 978-1-934389-79-9 |
| ISLAM FOR BEGINNERS | ISBN 978-1-934389-01-0 |
| JANE AUSTEN FOR BEGINNERS | ISBN 978-1-934389-61-4 |
| JUNG FOR BEGINNERS | ISBN 978-1-934389-76-8 |
| KIERKEGAARD FOR BEGINNERS | ISBN 978-1-934389-14-0 |
| LACAN FOR BEGINNERS | ISBN 978-1-934389-39-3 |
| LIBERTARIANISM FOR BEGINNERS | ISBN 978-1-939994-66-0 |
| LINCOLN FOR BEGINNERS | ISBN 978-1-934389-85-0 |
| LINGUISTICS FOR BEGINNERS | ISBN 978-1-934389-28-7 |
| LITERARY THEORY FOR BEGINNERS | ISBN 978-1-939994-60-8 |
| MALCOLM X FOR BEGINNERS | ISBN 978-1-934389-04-1 |
| MARX'S DAS KAPITAL FOR BEGINNERS | ISBN 978-1-934389-59-1 |
| MCLUHAN FOR BEGINNERS | ISBN 978-1-934389-75-1 |
| MORMONISM FOR BEGINNERS | ISBN 978-1-939994-52-3 |
| MUSIC THEORY FOR BEGINNERS | ISBN 978-1-939994-46-2 |
| NIETZSCHE FOR BEGINNERS | ISBN 978-1-934389-05-8 |
| PAUL ROBESON FOR BEGINNERS | ISBN 978-1-934389-81-2 |
| PHILOSOPHY FOR BEGINNERS | ISBN 978-1-934389-02-7 |
| PLATO FOR BEGINNERS | ISBN 978-1-934389-08-9 |
| POETRY FOR BEGINNERS | ISBN 978-1-934389-46-1 |
| POSTMODERNISM FOR BEGINNERS | ISBN 978-1-934389-09-6 |
| PRISON INDUSTRIAL COMPLEX FOR BEGINNERS | ISBN 978-1-939994-31-8 |
| PROUST FOR BEGINNERS | ISBN 978-1-939994-44-8 |
| RELATIVITY & QUANTUM PHYSICS FOR BEGINNERS | ISBN 978-1-934389-42-3 |
| SARTRE FOR BEGINNERS | ISBN 978-1-934389-15-7 |
| SAUSSURE FOR BEGINNERS | ISBN 978-1-939994-41-7 |
| SHAKESPEARE FOR BEGINNERS | ISBN 978-1-934389-29-4 |
| STANISLAVSKI FOR BEGINNERS | ISBN 978-1-939994-35-6 |
| STRUCTURALISM & POSTSTRUCTURALISM FOR BEGINNERS | ISBN 978-1-934389-10-2 |
| TESLA FOR BEGINNERS | ISBN 978-1-939994-48-6 |
| TONI MORRISON FOR BEGINNERS | ISBN 978-1-939994-54-7 |
| WOMEN'S HISTORY FOR BEGINNERS | ISBN 978-1-934389-60-7 |
| UNIONS FOR BEGINNERS | ISBN 978-1-934389-77-5 |
| U.S. CONSTITUTION FOR BEGINNERS | ISBN 978-1-934389-62-1 |
| ZEN FOR BEGINNERS | ISBN 978-1-934389-06-5 |
| ZINN FOR BEGINNERS | ISBN 978-1-934389-40-9 |